Also by William West

Psychotherapy and Spirituality: Crossing the Line between Therapy and Religion

Spiritual Issues in Therapy: Relating Experience to Practice

William West

palgrave
macmillan

First published 2004 by
PALGRAVE MACMILLAN
Houndmills, Basingstoke, Hampshire RG21 6XS and
175 Fifth Avenue, New York, N.Y. 10010
Companies and representatives throughout the world

PALGRAVE MACMILLAN is the global academic imprint of the Palgrave
Macmillan division of St. Martin's Press, LLC and of Palgrave Macmillan Ltd.
Macmillan® is a registered trademark in the United States, United Kingdom
and other countries. Palgrave is a registered trademark in the European
Union and other countries.

ISBN 0–333–99041–2

This book is printed on paper suitable for recycling and made from fully
managed and sustained forest sources.

A catalogue record for this book is available from the British Library.

A catalog record for this book is available from the Library of Congress.

10   9   8   7   6   5   4   3   2   1
13 12 11 10 09 08 07 06 05 04

Printed in China

This book is dedicated to: my late sister Elizabeth West (1948–2002) a woman of some spirit, and to my late father Harry West (1913–2003) a sailor and tentmaker.

Contents

List of Figures and Tables

Figures

Tables

Acknowledgements

A book such as this one is for many years in gestation. Wherever possible I have referenced and acknowledged the sources of the ideas and concepts. However, much of my deepest knowledge arises from interactions with people. In such a light I wish to value the part played by the following people: Linda Ankrah, Allen Bergin, Mary Berry, Dee Brown, Kam Dhillon, Christine Fremantle, the late Alan Gaskell, Peter Gubi, Judy Gaskell, Shari Geller, Henry Hollanders, Susan James, Grace Jantzen, Chris Jenkins, Nick Ladany, Pittu Laungani, Anne Littlewood, Jeanette Marsh, John McLeod, Jan Micthell, Lyn Myint-Maung, Roy Moodley, Fiona Moore, Clark Moustakas, Janet Muse-Burke, Greg Nolan, Marie O'Brien, David Orlinsky, Abdullah Popoola, David Rennie, Scott Richards, Wayne Richards, Rebecca Sima, Mike Sivori, Rob Spicer, Adriana Summers, Richard Summers, David Smith, Mansor Abu Talib, Brian Thorne, David Tune, the late Brian Wade and Dori Yusef.

During the incubation of this book I attended British Association for Counselling and Psychotherapy Annual Research Conferences at Bristol (2001), London (2002) and Leicester (2003), and the Society for Psychotherapy Research (International) Conferences in Montevideo (2001), Santa Barbara (2002) and Weimar (2003) that were, and are, marvellous places for germination. My PhD group of students remains a fertile setting for an ongoing debate around therapy, spirituality and culture.

My colleagues here at the University of Manchester have been especially accepting of my increasing eccentricity as this book has been writing itself. Apart from those mentioned above I wish to mention the unfailing humour and gate-keeping by Shelley Darlington that has been beyond the call of duty.

Finally the part played by my wife Gay and daughter Emily is beyond words.

Parts of this book have earlier appeared elsewhere in various guises but have been updated and woven into the fabric of this book.

I am, however, grateful for the opportunities given to air some of these ideas in: British Journal of Guidance and Counselling; Critical Journal of Psychology, Counselling and Psychotherapy; Counselling and Psychotherapy Research; The Friends' Quarterly; and the Newsletter of the Association for Pastoral and Spiritual Care and Counselling (APSCC).

Introduction

[There are times when] the best of therapy...leads to a dimension that is spiritual.
(Rogers quoted in Baldwin 2000 p. 35)

Ignorance is God's prison/Knowing is God's palace – Rumi.
(Barks 1995 p. 28)

Counselling and psychotherapy have an ongoing problem with spirituality. This happens despite the continued active interest of many people in their spiritual lives. This often involves an extended process of sense-making, sometimes of confusion, occasionally of deep distress all of which is, or could be the day-to-day area of work of the counsellor or psychotherapist.

Despite counselling and psychotherapy (as practised in the USA and Western Europe) being largely secularised, they have their roots in religious forms of soul care (McLeod 1998, West 2000a). Indeed, pastoral counsellors in Britain played a key part in the establishment of the British Association for Counselling and Psychotherapy as the professional body for counsellors and counselling (West 1998b). Many writers on counselling (e.g. Halmos 1965, McLeod 1998) have commented on how the decline in the number of clergy and pastoral care workers have matched the increases in counsellors. People are now more likely to turn to the counsellors rather than to the priest for help with their problems.

However, in this secularisation of counselling and psychotherapy it is felt in many quarters that something has been lost and that clients' spiritual needs are not always being effectively addressed within the talking therapies (Thorne 1991, 1998, 2002; West 2000a). Indeed counsellors in training are wanting more of a focus on spirituality (Swinton 1996, Davy 2001). Therapeutic techniques drawn from pastoral forms of care have not always been transferred effectively, if at all, over into secular counselling. Therapists often do effectively address clients' spiritual needs but the competence of any individual therapist in this area can vary according to the school of therapy they were trained in and their own inclinations (Rowan 1993).

In this book I explore the implications of the world of therapy addressing the reality of many people's active spirituality, drawing from my own experiences both as someone with a keen interest in spirituality, in researching therapy and spirituality, and also from my work with clients, individually, and groups within therapy, healing, religious and educational settings. This book represents a number of my current preoccupations and interests relating to therapy and spirituality that will be further explored in subsequent chapters. In brief these concerns are:

- the challenge of being present to our clients' spirituality and spiritual issues;
- making sense of what I refer to as psychospiritual therapeutic practice;
- the thorny question of cross-cultural work and learning from traditional healing;
- the challenge of researching therapy and spirituality;
- implications of this emerging way of working with clients which I have tentatively labelled soul attending.

A few examples from my own life and therapeutic practice should prove illuminating here:

1   A fairly recent client of mine, whom I call Matthew, told me during one therapy session of the 'spiritual resonance' he was experiencing with me and of how he was afraid of the 'spiritual intimacy' that was occurring between us (discussed in Chapter 5).
2   In a research email I am told, 'The practice of therapy always feels sacred to me. I consider the client's spiritual well-being and spiritual path, even if we do not discuss it as such. I consider the therapy room to be sacred space a sacred container for the issues of the soul. Generally I do not use this language with clients, however, it is my personal frame for the process.'
3   Recently I was in York for a meeting with counselling colleagues and having a few minutes to spare I decided to visit the Minster. As I entered the cathedral I immediately felt a sense of being in a spiritual place, if you like I was awestruck. I made for the small chapel that I knew was set aside for

silent prayer. Inside the chapel I was overwhelmed by the feel of the spiritual energy present and was moved to weep. I felt such a sense of gratitude at being able to feel this energy and also had a sense of being enabled to return to my true nature or spiritual self. This was immediately followed by a feeling of regret at not living enough from that true centre of mine. I spent some time in prayer for those close to me especially those in difficulties, and also spent time in contemplative silence. I left the Minster feeling uplifted and cleansed and somewhat washed out.

4   On another occasion I am working with a client who does not reveal much, is very contained in fact, I am feeling bored but know that this is not the full picture nor the end of his story. I suddenly have an image of a chained and beaten dog. It seems so off beam but in despair of making any kind of progress I share it with him. Out pours the story of being locked in the cupboard under the stairs by a crazy mother who would beat him and punish him in a seemingly random way so that he could not anticipate or adjust his behaviour to avoid the punishments.

5   On another time I am on a training course about healing and suddenly I notice that half the members of the group have red cones of light seemingly sat on their heads like dunces caps. Soon afterwards I am with some clients and see a peach colour around their heads just before they talk about their spirituality. With another, there is an orange colour just prior to pouring out the difficulties of their current sexual relationship.

What do these phenomena mean (apart from the obvious doubts the reader might have about my mental health and therapeutic practice!) and what implications does it have for my work as a therapist and for my life as a human being? This book explores the answers to these and other questions in the following chapters.

At this juncture it will help if I introduce, discuss and define some key concepts which I will be using through this book. These include spirituality, psychospirituality, unfolding and where I stand.

Spirituality

There are currently three definitions of spirituality that I find especially applicable to the psychospiritual territory of this book.

These are those of Elkins *et al.* (1988) who especially emphasise the impact of spirituality on the person, Rowan (1993) who points us to understanding the relationships of spirituality with our sense of self and beyond, and Swinton (2001) who is more focused on the person in relation to themselves, others and their community.

In many ways the Elkins *et al.* (1988) definition is the most impressive as it was the outcome of a research process aiming to define and understand spirituality from a humanistic phenomenological viewpoint. Their definition is 'Spirituality which comes from the Latin spiritus, meaning "breath of life" is a way of being and experiencing that comes through awareness of a transcendental dimension and that is characterized by certain identifiable values in regard to self, others, nature, life and whatever one considers to be the Ultimate' (Elkins *et al.* 1988 p. 10).

This definition can usefully be unpacked. They are talking about a way of being and experiencing, not a creed to be believed in but a life to be led. The mention of a transcendental dimension links us into the notion what spirituality can be, and often is, to do with altered states of consciousness. They also point us towards the values and ethics that are identified with an alive spirituality, if not always acted on.

Elkins and his team from their researches into spirituality identified it as having nine major components. They are:

1   *A transcendental dimension* exists and can be experienced whether as a personal God, a transcendent dimension, Greater Self and so on.
2   *Meaning and purpose in life*, that the 'existential vacuum' can be filled with an authentic life.
3   *Mission in life*, that the spiritual person has a vocation.
4   *Sacredness of life*, that life is infused with sacredness and the spiritual person can experience awe, reverence and wonder even in non-religious settings, and that all of life is holy.
5   *Challenging material values*, that ultimate satisfaction is to be found not in materials but in things of the spirit.
6   *Altruism*, being affected by the pain and suffering of others, having a sense of social justice and that we are all part of creation.
7   *Idealism*, having a vision of a better world and a desire to bring it about.

8   *Awareness of the tragic,* that pain, suffering and death are part of life and give it colour and shade.
9   *Fruits of spirituality,* that being truly spiritual changes all aspects of who we are and how we live.

Rowan's (1993) definition of something 'experienced as spiritual' clearly arises from his many years of transpersonal therapeutic practice and writing: 'Sometimes it may be experienced as inside ourselves: this is the typical experience of contacting the real self. Sometimes it may be experienced as outside ourselves: this is the typical experience of contacting the transpersonal self. Sometimes it may be experienced as a total letting-go: this is the typical experience of contacting the divine, which may be known as energy, as nature, as god or goddess, as pure being, as the void, or whatever' (p. 3). This definition is very useful in that it helps us locate our spiritual experiences either within the self, or the transpersonal self or beyond everything.

Swinton (2001) again from a seasoned practitioner, academic and writer's viewpoint offers us a definition: 'Spirituality is an intra, inter and transpersonal experience that is shaped and directed by the experience of individuals and of the communities within which they live out their lives. It is intrapersonal in that it refers to the quest for inner connectivity...It is interpersonal in that it relates to the relationships between people and within communities. It is transpersonal in so far as it reaches beyond self and others in the transcendent realms of experience that move beyond that which is available at a mundane level' (p. 20).

Bringing these three definitions together gives us a picture of what could be seen as an incarnate or embodied spirituality that engages the whole person including their soul or Higher Self and that is rooted in community. This is perhaps a very ambitious view that will not be readily achieved but it does offer us the vision of a healthy spirituality and gives us pointers to some of the likely therapeutic issues that can arise.

Psychospiritual

Some people insist that it is possible to separate the psychological out from the spiritual and thereby to have experts who deal with each part. Indeed this is a neat way of therapists dealing, or rather not dealing, with their uncomfortableness around spirituality and religion.

There is something to be said for specialism, indeed some of the successes of modern Western medicine have developed out of just this. However, we are holistic beings greater than sum of our parts and it is a challenge at times to decide whether a problem is physical, psychological or psychosomatic. If we then consider spirituality, the whole issue becomes even more difficult. Some thing, some essence of our humanness, gets lost if we go too far down this road, indeed many modern illnesses and troubles seem increasingly hard to categorise, and we can begin to see how illnesses are construed culturally (Gergen 1996). This is clearly apparent in the therapy world in which there are fashions in diagnosis. Every few years, we get a new label to attach to those troubled souls who do not quite fit existing categories. For example, borderline is a fairly recent one, previously schizoid was a popular label.

In discussing this issue of whether we can and should separate the psychological from the spiritual, Benner (1988) suggested that instead we speak of a 'psychospiritual unity'. This phrase was taken up by the human inquiry group (West 1996) that formed part of my doctoral studies and who chose to continue meeting in June 1994, calling itself the Psychospiritual Initiative (West 2000a). It should also be noted that there is a grouping of therapists who call themselves psychospiritual in contrast to using the word 'transpersonal' which is explored by Jones (1996) and others (Brazier 1996, Sills 1996, Whitmore 1996) in a special spiritual edition of the journal Self and Society.

I will therefore use this phrase 'psychospiritual' in a general sense to identify the territory of this book which is about working with clients' spirituality in a psychotherapeutic encounter. Clearly an increasing number of therapists are relating to their clients as spiritual beings, although a large number still do not, or at least not explicitly. Likewise there are many people in the world of pastoral care and spiritual direction who are also working psychospiritually with their clients but there are a number who work spiritually rather than psychospiritually. (I will return to this matter in the final chapter.)

Unfolding

A phrase I repeatedly use in this book is 'unfolding'. This is a concept and an understanding of a spiritual truth, maybe *the* spiritual truth that I have developed in dialogue with Richard Summers and Mary Swale though neither of them should be seen as responsible for how I use, or misuse it! The basic idea is that there is a spiritual unfolding for each of us and for part and all of creation that is waiting to happen. We can either allow it or block it. Certain spiritual practices like meditation, prayer and contemplation often allow it as many therapeutic practices do especially listening and empathy. It comes out of a place of *being*, of being with, or witnessing, of midwifery rather than a *doing*. It is not a passive non-active process; indeed unfolding can have a very dramatic aspect and very dramatic consequences. But it does seem as if we have to return repeatedly to the quiet centre at the heart of our souls to remember the deepest and fullest truth of who and how we really are and what our lives are meant to be about. I make no claims for the faithfulness of my own adherence to my unfolding. Fear and low self-esteem continue to restrict all that I could as does my ego. Nevertheless my best comes out of my truest link to this sense of spiritual unfolding and it serves to me as a useful way or concept for understanding other people's progress in therapy, pastoral care, and life as a whole. Perhaps it is always going to be an incompleted process, and perhaps that is why few of us are truly saints, may be the human condition is for most of us most of the time so designed that we fail, we do and we be less than what we truly are. Hence our searching, our spiritual practices, our therapies.

Having written these words by that familiar process of synchronicity, I read an article by Judy Clinton entitled 'Not enough love' in which she writes about the death of her son who was addicted to alcohol. She movingly tells us:

> My love had not been enough for my son; nor had the love of those who cared for him both personally and professionally. The *doing* had been enormous, the mental interactions and practical help had been many and varied, but the quality of *being* was actually what my son needed but did not encounter...The time when my son was most at peace with me – and therefore able to look constructively at his life – was when I myself was in a good, spiritually anchored place within myself. It was the greatest gift I could give him, but was so intent on 'fixing' his problems that I rarely reached that place of serenity which we both so sorely needed. I now believe that the only way we can touch people who are deeply distressed is through

the degree to which we can tap in to God's love – universal
energy.

(Clinton 2002 p. 13)

Where do I stand?

Therapeutically I work within a broadly humanistic-integrated
framework within a spiritual context. I am interested in our lived
experiences of spirituality rather than in the intricacies of theology (although that does have some attraction for me). I am
more than willing to discuss spiritual experiences in non-spiritual
terms, provided secular language used does effectively facilitate
such a discussion. This stance is not only applicable to my therapeutic work but also to my research and teaching and to my life
as a whole.

Opening out this frame further, I am drawn to a phenomenological viewpoint that is respectful of how you, another person,
experience life. Phenomenologically speaking, we can never know
reality directly (except perhaps for mystical experiences), all we
know is our perception of reality. Consequently my perception of
reality should not be considered more real than yours. Hopefully
I am not trying to 'normalise' you into accepting some kind of
group norm, group perception of reality, indeed it is the non-
normal that interests me! It should be apparent what profound
implications this has for how therapy is conducted, for the practice of the mental health services, with profound consequences
around mental health diagnosis. There is an interesting debate
(more of this later) about what is mystical, what is psychosis which
is often resolved in a white Eurocentric 'scientific' way at the expense
of white and non-white clients.

I also find something of value in a social constructionist view of
the world which 'regards personal experience and meaning as
being not merely created by the individual (the constructionist
position) but embedded in a culture and shaped by that culture'
(McLeod 1998 p. 152). That is, it is the stories we tell to ourselves
and to others about our world, that shape our lives, that experience
is socially constructed (Gergen 1985) and that the person can be
understood as a living 'text' (Gergen 1988) inhabiting a 'storied
world' (Sarbin 1986). In this context successful therapy could be
viewed as supporting our clients to give voice to a different story
or to frame an existing story in a new way. I am mindful of how

Linda Ankrah (2000, 2002), whose work is discussed in Chapter 4 was able to handle her own spiritual emergency through a study of Western therapists writing about spirituality and a study of writers on African spirituality. Phenomenology and social constructionistism lend themselves to a postmodernism view of the world (further discussed in Chapter 1) with its notion that the grand overarching narratives of early times no longer hold sway (e.g. Christianity, objective science, etc.) and that the gap has been filled by many local but often globally connected sub-cultures. Differences then become a source of interest and fascination rather than something to be rid of.

I know what I know and know that it is only provisional: I can never bracket completely, never in ordinary consciousness step out of all of the many assumptions – known and tacit – that guide and structure who I am, how I am, how I relate, how I think and feel. I know we can mostly agree on what is a table or what is a computer but I also know how unreliable eyewitness evidence is; that I see the colour of human auras and most people do not, that my dyed in the wool psychodynamic colleagues will never fully agree with their person-centred counterparts about human nature and other lesser matters. Maybe this sense of each of our uniquenesses however embedded in whatever cultures and sub-cultures allows the best possibility of working with, and being with, another person in a therapeutic encounter.

It has been suggested that my earlier book on therapy and spirituality (West 2000a) 'could be construed as anti-clerical' (Bond 2002 p. 44). This was not my actual intent though I do bear the pain of my own struggle with Christianity and with the Christian Church. I certainly was, and still am, critical of the Church of England for its non-acceptance of gay and lesbian relationships. This includes the dreadful response within the Church of England to the prospect of Canon Jeffrey John becoming Bishop of Reading. His celibacy was not enough for his opponents. The Church of England still cannot bear to make women bishops. These issues point to a deeper malaise and to a huge gap between the more tolerant, in some ways more 'Christian' largely secular British society and the Church of England itself. As I write this, I read of the Pope's recent proclamation (*The Guardian* 22 August 2003) on the 'evil' of homosexual marriages. It is enough to make Jesus weep!

Having wrestled for years with what Jesus Christ meant to me, I found spiritual peace among the Religious Society of Friends (Quakers) who, despite their Christian origins (Dandelion 1996), do not have a fixed creedal view of Christ which all have to subscribe to. Indeed there are clearly many Quakers who are not Christians. A key feature of Quakerism that I found most attractive is its focus on how we experience spirituality and on our need to wrestle with what it means to us. It also operates on a clear commitment to equality and, in Britain, on having no pastors or priests. There are many features of this approach that overlap with therapy, especially with person-centred therapy (West 1995b).

However, in recent years despite being a Quaker I have on occasion, when it felt right, taken Holy Communion within the Church of England. (This is a sacred ritual central to the practice of Christianity in which wine and bread are blessed by a priest in the name of Christ and then eaten and drunk by those present, able and willing to.)

Besides these links to Christianity and Quakerism I spent most of my 30s in a New Age spiritual context, not linked to any particular group but actively engaged in regular meditation and healing rituals, and influenced by a number of different spiritual and religious currents including, in particular, contact with Buddhist teachings and various forms of feminist theology. There seemed to be a thin line in those days (1980s) between humanistic therapy and spirituality, or at least in the circles I moved in.

Another critic of my earlier book thought that I overemphasised the joy of the spiritual journey. In fact a key motivation behind my writings around spirituality and therapy is to give voice to that which I feel is not being said. My readings around pastoral care (e.g. Guenther 1992, Jeff 1987, Leech 1994, Lyall 1995) left me feeling that the sheer joy and awe of the spiritual experience had been insufficiently expressed. In this book I do refer to the 'dark night of the soul', that sense of being completely deserted by God, when life has little or no meaning. However, my own frequent experience of contemplation and prayer is that of feeling blessed, to borrow a phrase from Matthew Fox (1993) 'original blessing' (though I would not claim to follow all of Fox's theology). It is not that I do not know suffering, it is just that I still feel blessed despite it. This of course may owe everything to my childhood or my genetics. Maybe it is all just a matter of how we are wired or miswired, but I do not think so.

What this book is and what it is not?

This book explores how psychotherapy and counselling can address the everyday aspects of human spirituality that arise for therapy clients. Indeed it views the therapeutic encounter as innately and at the very least implicitly spiritual. The book also considers the impact of addressing spiritual issues on the therapist and on therapeutic models and theories. It is written from a basically humanistic integrative position (West 2000c) that is welcoming of the client's spirituality. It is not a theological book as such though it may well reflect my own interests and biases in that area. There is much in this book of relevance to those engaged in pastoral care and counselling, indeed to anyone involved or interested in all forms of care, professional or lay, which seek to be inclusive of spirituality.

What is in this book?

Chapter 1 sets the scene, exploring therapy in the postmodern world. It poses the question: why spirituality and spiritual experiences remain a taboo within the therapy world, and discusses the rise of therapy as a secular activity, the legacy of Freud, the decline of traditional religion, and the reality of human spirituality. Chapter 2 invites us to re-frame our view of psychotherapy by locating it within a tradition of shamanic healing, in which the originators of a number of modern schools of psychotherapy like Freud, Jung, Reich and possibly Rogers show signs of a creative or initiatory illness which is a key feature of shamanic emergence.

Chapter 3, the personal encounter with spirituality explores how aspects of our spiritual and therapeutic journey can illuminate spirituality and therapy. This includes times of faith, doubt, visions and despair, with examples drawn from people's stories, my researches and own experiences. This chapter also focuses on the question of what is the truth of mysticism and spiritual experiences, and also whether religion is to be seen as inner experience or outward behaviour. Chapter 4, making sense of the territory, puts forward some maps and other ways of making sense of the psychospiritual realm and includes comments on considering therapy itself as a faith journey.

Chapter 5 focuses on the clients' story, and asks: are they seeking psychological change/adjustment or gnosis? It poses the question of how to support the spiritual process within the client, and what difficulties can arise. Chapter 6 addresses some especially relevant spiritual and therapeutic issues. It considers the possibilities of spiritual interventions in therapy and pastoral care before focusing on forgiveness as one such intervention, which was the subject of some recent research by myself and a colleague (West 2001b). Bereavement counselling which frequently addresses spirituality is then explored, followed by the role of retreats, which is a form of pastoral care that has spiritual and therapeutic implications. Finally the context of spiritually inclined is explored.

Chapter 7 is concerned with researching spirituality and therapy. How to systematically research therapy and spirituality whilst remaining true to the territory and asking the awkward, the obvious and naïve questions. Inner data analysis is proposed as part of a process of remaining spiritually alive in research. The final chapter is entitled 'Soul Attending' and it pulls together the threads of this book, pointing us towards the new type of psychospiritual practitioner now emerging. Various elements of the life on the spiritually awake therapist working with psychospirituality are explored, including: use of language, soul attending, spiritual self care, appropriate supervision, courageous heart and soul, acting ethically, necessary knowledge and living the spiritual life as a therapist.

Gender, race and culture

Whilst great efforts have been made to use inclusive language and thinking in this book so as to avoid racist, sexist, class, religious and cultural biases, the task of dealing with tacit and unconscious biases is much harder to complete. Inevitably I am a creature of my culture and sub-cultures that must filter and shape my thinking and feeling and above all my spirituality.

Chapter 1
The Context

The separation, if not opposition, between psychoanalysis and religion is the essence of the naturalistic explanations of psychoanalysis. Religion is nonadmissible given its assumptions of transcendence and theology.

(Payne *et al.* 1992)

This chapter sets the scene exploring therapy in the postmodern world. It then considers why spirituality and spiritual experiences remain a taboo within the therapy world, the rise of therapy as a secular activity, the legacy of Freud, the decline of traditional religion and the reality of human spirituality.

Therapy in a postmodern world

With the death of God, proclaimed by Nietzsche at the turn of the century, man came to be the measure of all things, and psychology became the secularised religion of modernity. In modernity the loss of a belief in an absolute God had been succeeded by the modernist declaration of faith: "I believe in one objective reality."

(Kvale 1992 p. 53)

Postmodernism is the consequence of the failures of the program of modernism.

(Polkinghorne 1992 p. 147)

The assumption of modernity was that humankind could and would progress through reason and science. By 1945 after the horrendous carnage of two world wars and the dropping of the atom bombs on Japan, modernity has lost its appeal. Einstein and other physicians had turned Newtonian physics on its head, including the realisation that the observer could not be separated from the observed.

According to Kvale (1992) in the 1950s the concept of postmodernism was beginning to appear in architecture, literary criticism and sociology mostly in the USA and was further developed by French philosophers in the 1970s, beginning to come into general usage in the 1980s. 'Postmodern thought is characterised by a loss of belief in an objective world and an incredibility towards metanarratives of legitimation' (Kvale 1992 p. 32).

Polkinghorne (1992) explored how much postmodern concepts could be found in the practice of 12 experienced US therapists. He found that the concepts of:

• *Foundationlessness* – use of a diverse range of theories whether eclectically or integratively (most therapists are probably not 'pure school' any more) (Hollanders 1997, 2000, Hollanders and McLeod 1997).

• *Fragmentariness* – uniqueness of each client; therefore each intervention is tailor made, one size does not fit all, cannot make generalisations about gender, race and culture.

• *Constructivism* – human experience is a construction; understanding our clients is constructed against a choice and mix of theories.

• *Neopragmatism* – successful therapists adjust their practice in response to client responses driven by pragmatics rather than theory.

All these were applicable to both postmodern thought and to the practice of his therapists. Leaving aside the challenge that he found what he was looking for and also that therapeutic theory and practice inevitably reflects the culture it is found in his research may well be telling us why therapy is so popular in the modern Western world. Indeed Lynch (1999) suggests that the growth of the counselling movement itself is understandable in the context of a postmodern society. Lynch directs us towards Toulmin (1990) who identified four characteristics of modernism that have been reversed by postmodernism. These are: the written over the oral; the universal over the particular; the general over the local; and the timelessness over the timely.

McLeod (1997) relates modern therapy to some key features of postmodernism: globalisation, reflexivity, and replacement of 'grand narratives' by 'local knowledges'. He points that just as psychotherapy was beginning to establish itself as a rational research-based discipline it finds that many of its most exciting developments are coming from innovations in therapeutic practice (and I would add research) that have drawn on feminism, political activism, religion and spiritual practice, and indigenous healing rituals. McLeod concludes: 'The postmodern impulse is to deconstruct therapy, to strip away its claim to privileged scientific knowledge/power/certainty and to reveal the core of therapy as an arena for telling personal stories' (1997 p. 23).

Postmodernism has not been without its critics including those from within the therapy world such as Howard 'Postmodern philosophy, at its worse, presumes no authority at all except to claim with authority that there are no authorities. This kind of talk has no future.' (2000 p. 365). Laungani (2003) is very scathing when it comes to postmodernism which he insists defies an acceptable definition. He reminds us that 'modern' which comes from a Latin adverb literally means just now, so that postmodern means beyond just now! He suggests that the recent influx of people from differing cultural backgrounds into Britain coupled with globalisation and the Internet does not change the truth that it is not an easy task for people of different cultures to understand each other. He comments: 'The cultural mix seen from the outside conveys the impression of assimilation, even integration. But behind closed doors, when each individual enters his/her own home, the apparent similarity ends, and life takes of a specific culture-centred dimension.'

There are those who claim that we are now in the post postmodern era. The massive demand for therapy points to a malaise which traditional religion seems to have no answer to, which highlights the limitations of modernity. Successful therapy, and there seems to be a lot of it about, is based on hope, on a good enough therapeutic relationship, on active listening, on helping the client make sense of their world, despite the failures of the 'grand narratives'. If such work is postmodern, so be it. As Lynch (1999) points out, there is still room for spirituality and religion in the postmodern world. Maybe there is a possibility of a true humility, a lack of grandiosity when the grand narratives die out.

There are a number of aspects of postmodern life that I feel are of benefit and are to be welcomed. These include:

- its respecting of other's reality;
- its valuing of the local;
- its linking into the global via the Internet and other means;

- the Internet is implicitly postmodern;
- its sense of culture as an ongoing process of creation which we can all participate in;
- implicit and often explicit deep equality of cultures and faiths;
- valuing of the individual's authoring of their own life;
- fluidity which can at its best be creative and innovative, at worse chaotic;
- emphasis on evaluation by one's peer community; and
- its refusal to close down the debate, hence a lack of 'control freakery'.

There are some very clear overlaps with many of the above statements and the practice of therapy, especially humanistic therapy with its respect for the client's reality but also with qualitative research with its emphasis on local knowledge. A postmodern view of life whilst potentially frustrating in its refusal of authority and traditional hierarchy does represent, I believe, a useful framework within which to consider and locate spirituality in Britain today. It is perhaps more valid to see our society as post-Christian, a society which still privileges the Christian narrative. However Christianity itself is in decline and the largest spiritual grouping would have to be New Age or unaligned. I do not honestly believe we can get back to a massive adherence to Christianity despite the hopes of many evangelical Christians. Indeed I do not think a resurgence of Christianity in that form would be a spiritual step forward.

Therapy and spirituality

For many psychotherapists and counsellors, the question of whether they are effectively trained to deal with issues relating to their clients, spirituality is very much a hit-or-miss affair. A number of courses will briefly touch on spirituality and/or religion as an optional part of the course or deal with it within time set aside for cross-cultural issues. Either way it receives insufficient coverage which I think might well reflect limitations and biases amongst the trainers. Such poor coverage does not reflect the students' viewpoint (Swinton 1996) but it does seem to reflect a tension around spirituality and religion that goes back to the origins of modern therapy.

Modern therapy could be said to have begun with Freud. Some of the ideas that Freud popularised were around at the time but he also innovated clinically and developed his theories from his practice. Freud was a non-practising Jew but in many ways his therapeutic persona owed a lot to the image of the Rabbi – therapist as expert, therapist as interpreter. Freud also wrestled with the idea of religion returning to it again and again. However, like many educated people of his time (late 19th to early 20th century) Freud was against religion and indeed wished to be seen as a scientist.

Clearly modern science, medicine and psychology had to be free of religious control in order to develop but this antagonism between the two served therapy badly and continues to be problematic. One consequence was that modern therapy developed without awareness or acknowledgement of its roots in various forms of soul care (McLeod 1998, West 2000a). Another consequence was that Freud had a negative view of religion, seeing it as at best a 'crooked cure' (quoted in Hay 1982) and at worst as 'infantile' (Freud 1963).

This view of Freud's still holds sway for many therapists and it relates deeply to the question of what is the good life? Who is a healthy person? For Freud 'the purpose of life is simply the programme of the pleasure principle' (1963 p. 13). For others the good life invariably involves addressing issues of religion and spirituality. Jung was less taken by Freud's focus on sexuality as the cause and cure of human suffering and looked more towards spirituality as a necessary part of human happiness. Jung memorably states 'among my patients in the second half of life – that is over 35 years of age – there has not been a single one whose problem has not been in the last resort that of finding a religious outlook on life' (1933 p. 164). If we were to take these words of Jung's seriously they would transform our modern psychotherapeutic practice, putting the spirituality of our clients at the heart of the therapeutic encounter.

This question of what is the good life, can be seen as guiding our work as therapists, both implicitly and explicitly. Gordon Lynch has explored this question very effectively within the realm of pastoral care and counselling (Lynch 2002). It is clear that many therapists and especially their trainers and schools have defined the good life to exclude religion and spirituality and thereby any focus on spirituality will be framed around it being seen as neurotic or pathological.

Within Britain the Christian Churches are largely in decline from what was estimated to be 27 per cent of the adult population in 1850, declining to 14 per cent in 1990 (Bruce 1995b). Current figures are even lower, Brierley (2000) notes that regular church attendance in Britain fell from, 4.74 million in 1989 to 3.71 million in 1998; a drop of more than 20 per cent in ten years. Less than 8 per cent of the population are likely to be in church on an average Sunday. The congregations in the Church of England and Methodists are increasingly elderly. There are part of the Christian Churches that are growing especially the evangelical churches and the black churches.

This decline in what was the dominant religion masks several relevant features of spirituality in Britain today:

1   The role religion plays among ethnic minority groups. The Black Christian Churches are increasing in size, and there is an increasing number of mosques and Sikh, Hindu and Buddhist temples being built.

2   Non-Christian religions are increasing. For example, the Pagan Federation claims to be the fastest growing religion in Britain with over 100,000 followers.

3   New Religious Movements, a number of which are Christian but many are not, whose followers tend to be young and grouped around a charismatic leader.

4   New Age Spirituality sometimes referred to as Do-It-Yourself spirituality by its critics is a largely uncentralised but very popular form of religious expression that overlaps with some forms of therapy including humanistic and transpersonal therapies.

5   A huge number of people are actively involved in mediation without necessarily being signed up to one religion or another. There has been a large dissemination of spiritual practices like meditation and yoga in recent years.

Clearly any discussion of the role of spirituality in people's lives in modern Britain needs to look beyond what is happening in the Christian Churches. From this perspective perhaps, there has been no decline in the numbers of people actively engaged in spiritual practices since Victorian times.

David Hay (Hay and Morisy 1978, Hay 1982) did research into what he referred to as religious, ecstatic or paranormal experiences.

Via an opinion poll survey, he posed the question: 'Have you ever been aware of being influenced by a presence or power, whether referred to as God or not, which was different from your everyday self?' One-third of the people questioned answered 'Yes'. Hay (1979, 1982) then conducted some qualitative interviews in which the figure rose to two out of three replying 'Yes', which points to the taboo against such disclosure. Many of those questions said that this was the first time they had ever discussed such experiences since they feared being considered mad, if they did speak out. In his most recent study (Hay and Hunt 2000) Hay presents the figures listed in Table 1.1.

Notice that 76 per cent of those questioned now say 'Yes' to at least one of his questions about religious or spiritual experience. Hay concludes: not that people are having such experiences more but that they are now more willing to disclose them. He tells us that such experiences seem to be universal, and correlate with good health. There is some correlation with Church attendance but many people having such experiences do not attend. He regards such experiences as being biological and cross-cultural, and he speculates that they are a necessary part of our survival as a species otherwise they would have died out. This connects with Elkins *et al.*'s (1988) researches that point us to the shift away from materialism towards altruism that occurs for people having spiritual experiences.

TABLE 1.1   Frequency of report of religious or spiritual experience in Britain for the years 1987 and 2000, from Hay and Hunt (2000)

	1987(%)	2000(%)
A patterning of events	29	55
Awareness of the presence of God	27	38
Awareness of prayer being answered	25	37
Awareness of a sacred presence in nature	16	29
Awareness of the presence of the dead	18	25
Awareness of an evil presence	12	25
Cumulative total	48*	76

*This total includes respondents to two additional questions asked in 1987 about 'a presence not called God' (22 per cent) and 'awareness that all things are One (5 per cent), that is, the total of 76 per cent for the year 2000 is quite likely to be, relatively speaking, an underestimate.

In the context of this book the most recent research by David Hay (Hay and Hunt 2000) is especially relevant. In focus groups and individual research conversations with 31 people who saw themselves as religious or spiritual but who did not attend church (i.e. this group did not include people who no longer attended synagogue, temples or mosques) their key findings were:

- how very timid these people were about talking about religion and spirituality until they trusted the researchers' motives (i.e. not evangelising them!) and heard something of the researchers' own spiritual lives;
- the word 'spiritual' is clearly not in ordinary currency or well understood and might be linked to spiritualism or taken as not meaning religious;
- that their spirituality has a sense of a quest or journey;
- believe in a generic God rather than the Trinitarian God of Christianity;
- their idea that there is 'something there' that is hard to articulate in positive statements about spiritual experiences;
- they have self-constructed theologies often using fragments of what Hay calls 'the Christian meta-narrative'; and
- theodicy – the challenging question of 'if God is so powerful why does he not intervene more to relieve human suffering?'

Given that most people no longer attend the Christian Churches, but who could be located culturally as post-Christian, these are the kind of issues and themes around for the many who have a sense of spirituality however ill-defined and who may end up in the therapy room.

The truth of mysticism and spiritual experiences

Is a particular mystical experience 'true' or 'real'? In conversation with a colleague recently who is well informed on these matters, I was appalled by his criticism of Julian of Norwich's 'showings' as 'psychotic'. Julian of Norwich, who Brian Thorne suggests could be regarded as the patron saint of counsellors, was a medieval mystic who had a seemingly near-death experience in which a number of visions or what she called 'showings' came to her which she then spent the next 20 years in deciphering whilst living as an anchorite. It is the power of these 'showings' coupled with her commentary on them that makes Julian such a remarkable medieval mystic. Grace Jantzen (1987) achieved the remarkable feat of making Julian's writings especially relevant to our modern world. My friend's attitude to Julian neatly illustrates the whole vexed questions of what is true mysticism and the difficulty faced by any of us in distinguishing between mysticism and psychosis.

There is a real challenge which none of us can ever completely achieve of being open to the other person's experience, or at least their descriptions in words of their experiences and their behaviours resulting from their experiences, and then attempting to discern or make some kind of assessment of the health or otherwise of what they relate to us. But how do we tell whether the spiritual states, spiritual or mystical experiences of our clients or friends even are healthy?

This is deeply problematic. First of all we need to acknowledge that any kind of mental health, psychiatric, or psychotherapeutic diagnosis is intrinsically different to a physical diagnosis. For instance many of us would agree what was a broken leg if we saw one, we might disagree as to the best treatment but the diagnosis would be fairly reliable. Mental health diagnoses are plagued by fashions (e.g. schizoid used to be a very common diagnosis in the 1960s, then it was personality disorder, currently it is probably borderline personality disorder that is the latest catch of all); by ethnicity (people from some ethnic minority groups are over repre-sented in our mental hospital population); and by gender (are women really madder than men or do we just imprison difficult men and hospitalise difficult women?).

Gergen (1996) persuasively argues that mental diagnoses are the creation of a powerful club of practitioners who once they create a new one category suddenly find that plenty of their patients qualify for it. Such diagnosis is always done by the expert who often belongs to a different culture in many ways from his or her patient in a consultation in which the patient or client is not relaxed, not their usual self in a power relationship in which some subtle or gross coercion will apply and so on. We know from Allman et al.'s (1992) research work on mystical experiences that there appears to be a depressingly high level of misdiagnosis by psychotherapists. Some therapists, usually humanistic, could not see the difficulties present, having too rosy a few of mystical states whilst those of a more psychodynamic and Cognitive-Behavioural Therapy (CBT) bent would not sufficiently acknowledge that which is healthy is such experiences. One is left feeling that the diagnosis has been made before the patient enters the consulting room on the basis of a previously acquired prejudice.

So how can this dilemma be resolved? The work of Lukoff (Lukoff 1985; Lukoff *et al*. 1992, discussed more fully in West 2000a) is helpful here. Lukoff (1985) put forward a useful proposed DSM IV (i.e. Diagnostic and Statistical Manual of Mental Disorders, fourth edition) category that helpfully distinguishes between mystical states, psychotic states, mystical states with psychotic features and psychotic states with mystical features. This could be seen as a spectrum with pure mysticism at one end and psychosis at the other with varying mixtures in between. However, this presupposes that we accept the concept of psychosis which is open to debate. Lukoff's suggestions and discussion about what support people would likely need according to where on the spectrum their experience seems to lie is crucial. The emphasis then being on the support needs of the person involved rather than merely the intricacies of diagnosis.

In the post-September 11 time of a war against terrorism it is not possible to talk about healthy spirituality and spiritual experience without regard to the religious context in which this war is being raged. Whether we see this in the use of the word 'evil' attached to some states by President Bush or in the widespread Islamophobia in the West, or the use of religion on both sides of the Northern Ireland conflict, it is clear that to be religiously motivated is not at all always a good thing. Grace Jantzen was not well received when she pointed this out recently at an academic conference on religious experience, 'In the twenty-first century religion is conscripted on all sides to the service of oppression, terror and destruction. But is there also a variety of religious experience that works on the side of justice and of peace?' (2002 p. 2).

Religion as inner experience or outward behaviour

This brings us to the question of what is true religion: Is it the inner experiences we have that have the potential to lead us and teach us the spiritual life we are to follow, or is it that which can be seen or even measured in our outward behaviour? Can we really lead a full spiritual life without both? William Penn in the late 17th century thought they, spiritually minded people, should be in the world not in retreat from it and he talked about how true religion leads a man into the world rather than away from it. Wordsworth famously saw nature as his great moral teacher as a child and he was clearly taken up by mystical experiences occurring out in the open. He also wrote of how children come trailing clouds of glory having a connection with their spiritual origins that is often lost subsequently.

Allport (Allport and Ross 1967) offers us the useful distinction that can be made between intrinsic or mature religion and extrinsic or immature religion. Extrinsic persons use religion for their own ends and appear to turn towards God but without turning away from their self. The intrinsic, in contrast embrace a creed, indeed live their religion following it as fully as they can. I suspect these are either end of a spectrum with most spiritually minded people at varying points on the spectrum, points which are likely to change over time. Clearly intrinsically religious persons will have a religious faith and attitude that is in harmony with their inner experience of spirituality and vice versa though it is important to acknowledge how organised religions have often had great difficulties with their mystically inclined believers over the centuries.

The chapter began by considering therapy in a postmodern world before exploring the relationship between therapy and spirituality, relating it to Freud's view of religion and finally touching on spirituality in Britain today. We then considered the vexed question of mystical and spiritual experiences and the difficulties in separating out such experiences from psychosis especially when both could be present. Soul attending, a truly holistic approach to psychotherapy requires an ability by the practitioner of being unafraid to engage in these deep levels of human experience, guided in many ways by a knowledge of her or his own depth, however painfully acquired.

Chapter 2

Psychotherapists as Shaman

Historically, modern dynamic psychotherapy derives from primitive medicine, and an uninterrupted continuity can be demonstrated between exorcism and magnetism, magnetism and hypnotism, and hypnotism and the modern dynamic schools.

(Ellenberger 1970 p. 48)

The modern psychotherapist... relies to a large extent on the same psychological mechanisms used by the faith healer, shaman, physician, priest and others, and the results, as reflected by the evidence of therapeutic outcomes, appear to be substantially similar.

(Strupp 1972 p. 277)

This chapter begins by considering the phenomenon of shaman, the traditional healers of aboriginal societies. However, increasingly the concept of the shaman is being applied to Western therapists sometimes denoted as neo-shamanism to distinguish it from aboriginal shaman. One aspect of the emergence of the traditional healer or shaman was the phenomenon of creative or initiatory illness. This certainly can be seen in the biography of a number of psychotherapists. I have chosen to explore this with reference to some key psychotherapists, including Freud, Reich, Jung, Horney and Rogers. I then consider its application to those I have researched.

Shamanism

Walsh (1994) provides a definition of shamanism that captures many of its key elements succinctly: 'a family of traditions whose practitioners focus on voluntary entering altered states of consciousness in which they experience themselves or their spirit(s) traveling to other realms at will and interacting with other entities to serve their community' (p. 9).

Walsh (1994) further clarifies that his definition distinguishes shamanism from mere psychopathological states and also from religious practices since the focus of the shaman's work is that of healing a person, family or community. According to Walsh (1994) his deliberate use of altered states and of interacting with other entities distinguishes shamanism from medicine men and priests who do not usually enter altered states (Winkelman 1989) and from mediums who do have altered states but who do not usually journey to other realms.

Shaman are usually 'called' to be shaman in dreams, visions, unusual experiences, omens and so on. The response to the call is often ambivalent but in shamanic societies there is a recognition that it cannot be resisted or some awful fate and possibly death will result. Later the initiation crisis will occur usually soon after adolescence. This can involve 'an onslaught of unusual psychological experiences... the shaman-to-be exhibits unusual... bizarre, dangerous, and life-threatening behavior. The results may be a period of weeks, months, or even years of unpredictable chaos that disrupts the lives of the shaman, the family, and the tribe' (Walsh 1994 pp. 12–13). The illness will often be recognised by the community or tribe as a sign that the person is in the process of becoming a shaman and they will usually be sent to a shaman for training which can last for many years.

Rebecca Sima (2002) describes a Tanzanian woman brought up as a Christian and therefore hostile to traditional healing. Her initiation involved illnesses within her family rather than for herself. The woman felt the call to be a healer before formal schooling began: 'It all started like a miracle, because at eleven I could sit with my mother and tell many things that have not yet happened but will happen... Sometimes I could even tell if a person is going to die in the family or community. To our surprise all what I said could come true' (p. 153). There were consequences of this gift: 'many people in my village started consulting me to tell what could happen to them and sometimes requested me to help resolve their problems they encountered' (p. 153). She ended up giving people herbs to heal them and had dreams about how she could help those who consulted her. She felt ambivalent about this healing work because it 'interfered with my Christianity and modernity especially as I grew up in school' (p. 153). Indeed at her boarding school many strange things happened to her that frightened her, her fellow students and her teachers. She thought that by devoting herself to Christianity, the spirits would leave her alone and in fact she became a nun.

Over the next five years five of her siblings died strangely from unusual illnesses. 'It was believed that the siblings' deaths were punishments from the healing spirits, which were angry with the family, which behaved rudely as they did not advise me to obey what the spirits ordered me to do' (p. 153). Her father visited her and 'explained to me that all what had transpired in the family was due to my resistance to obey the ancestors' (p. 153). Having also taken advice from her extended family which agreed with her father's viewpoint she left the convent, and 'I could not only practice traditional healing but also get chance to marry and extend our family especially [given] that many of the siblings had died. We had to look for ways to retain the remaining members and extend the family. I married and had children' (p. 153). She describes what a 'difficult' decision this was for her. Interestingly she also trained as a nurse and has worked as both a nurse and a traditional healer for over 30 years. She talks of the value in being able to offer traditional healing to those unable to benefit from Western medicine.

It may seem difficult to understand a culture in which the ancestorial spirits have such a sway, such an influence on modern life. However, Lévi-Strauss (1966) cautions us that belief in such spirits does not imply a lack of logic or rationality given the assumptions widespread in that tribal culture, such behaviour is culturally appropriate. The challenge faced by the woman above that Sima (2002) explores at length, is when such a culture meets up with the Western culture. Sima found that the Western-trained counsellors in Tanzania were modifying their practice and being more directive and advice-giving than their Western counterparts and Western training were. Such counsellors were often contemptuous of traditional healers. Nevertheless most people in Tanzania still live in villages and consult traditional healers.

The outcome of the initiatory crisis, vividly described above, which can be considered a culturally specific developmental crisis to the shaman who will often function exceptionally well as a leader and healer of his people. The shaman is 'not only a sick man [but] he is a sick man who has been cured, who has succeeded in curing himself' (Eliade 1964 p. 27).

Links have been made between shamanism in aboriginal societies and the modern Western world (Ellenberger 1970, Rogers 1980, Willis 1992a,b, Pietroni 1993), and between shamanism and modern psychotherapy (Peters and Price-Williams 1980, Pendzik 1988, Krippner 1992). This has led some therapists to study ancient healing techniques including those of the Native American Indians and workshops and individual sessions are now offered in shamanism and neo-shamanism. Traditionally in most shamanic cultures shaman were chosen, they did not choose to become shaman. Indeed anyone seeking to become a shaman was usually regarded as less powerful than their chosen counterparts.

Creative illnesses

The ancient tradition that shaman become healers after passing through a deep seated initiatory or creative illness has been discussed in the modern British context by Roy Willis (1992a,b) and is well explored by Ellenberger (1970), who related it to modern psychotherapy. Ellenberger suggests that the illness occurs after a period of intense preoccupation with an idea and a search for truth. It can involve depression, neurosis, psychosomatic complaints or even psychosis. The intensity of the illness will vary but the preoccupation remains. The individual is self-absorbed and may feel utterly isolated despite what support she or he receives. The end of the illness is often rapid with feelings of elation. The person is very changed as a result of the experience and claims to have discovered a new possibly spiritual truth.

In my own researches into counsellors and psychotherapists whose work includes healing, I found that eight out of the thirty people I interviewed in depth had had some serious illness prior to their work assuming more of a healing nature. I discuss their experiences below. I will also in particular focus on some key experiences from the lives of Freud, Jung, Reich, Horney and Rogers as exemplars of those who founded schools of psychotherapy and faced their own demons in some form or other.

In the context of this book we should note that Freud never adopted a wholly positive view of spirituality, that Reich was very critical of organised religion but became increasingly receptive in the final years of his life. Jung was very positive about spirituality but not so enamoured with organised religion and Rogers became truly accepting of the spiritual only in the final years of his life. I am aware that I am largely focusing on male founders of psychotherapy schools and that there are other females besides Karen Horney who could be considered (e.g. Melanie Klein who only found any real relief from her depression in her thirties in analysis with Karl Abraham (Segal 1992)) and that the experience of a creative illness does equally involve females as my research discussed below bears out. The dominance of males in founding and leading psychotherapy schools remains an issue even though there are increasing numbers of women training and practising as psychotherapists.

Freud's illness

The strange malady that Sigmund Freud underwent between 1894 and 1900, together with his self-analysis, have given rise to various interpretations. Some of his adversaries contend that he was a seriously ill man, and psychoanalysis was the expression of a neurosis...It is our hypothesis that Freud's self-analysis was one aspect of a complex process (the others being his relationship with Fliess, his neurosis, and the elaboration of psychoanalysis), and that this process was an example of what may be called a creative illness.

(Ellenberger 1970 p. 447)

Freud had been preoccupied since 1886 with the origins of neurosis and he felt repeatedly that he was on the verge of discovering a great secret or truth. Freud also felt very isolated and intolerant of criticism. Fliess became a new mentor or in Ellenberger's words 'shaman master' or 'spiritual director' with Freud as shaman apprentice or mystic. Freud's creative illness ended with his discovery of the psychoanalytic method and his publication of his key book *The Interpretation of Dreams* in 1900.

Freud's biographer Ernest Jones writes: 'There is ample evidence that for ten years or so – roughly comprising the nineties [i.e. 1890s – WW] – he [Freud] suffered from a very considerable neurosis' (1953 p. 334). This took the form of 'alternations of mood... between periods of elation, excitement and self confidence on the one hand and periods of severe depression, doubt and inhibition on the other...Sometimes there were spells where consciousness would be greatly narrowed: states difficult to describe, with a veil that produced almost a twilight condition of mind' (1953 p. 336).

Despite an intense relationship with Fleiss conducted mostly via an extraordinary correspondence (Freud destroyed Fleiss' letters to him but his to Fleiss remain) by 1897 that, in many ways therapeutic, relationship was not working so well and Freud undertook his own self-analysis with a key focus on interpreting his own dreams. Jones tells us that 'for three or four years the neurotic suffering and dependence actually increased in intensity' (1953 p. 352). At one point Freud wrote to Fleiss, 'I believe I am in a cocoon, and God knows what kind of beast will creep out of it' (1953 p. 357).

From his own self-analysis Freud learnt so much about his clients' processes, in a letter to Fleiss (October 1897) he comments: 'Everything that I experience with patients I find here: days when I slink about oppressed because I have not been able to understand anything of my dreams, my phantasies and the moods of the day, and then again days in which a flash illuminates the connections and enables one to comprehend what has gone before as a preparation for to-day's vision' (Jones 1953 p. 359).

Freud's intense self-analysis, which in many ways was the basis for his book *The Interpretation of Dreams* – many of the dreams were Freud's own – became the model for his future work with clients and for his new 'science' of psychoanalysis. In a sense Freud's self-analysis never finished for he would devote the last half-hour of each day to that purpose.

Reich's madness

It seems highly likely that a creative illness also happened to Wilhelm Reich who entered a sanatorium in 1927 suffering from TB. Reich had become Freud's favourite son in the period following the First World War in Vienna but like many favourite sons developed some sort of rebellion against his father. By 1927 Reich was apparently suffering from depression due to Freud's reaction to his work and Freud's refusal to take him on as a client. Reich's younger brother died of TB in 1926 and there were problems within Reich's marriage. His wife Annie suggested that about that time he changed from being 'normal' to being more angrier and suspicious and showed signs of a psychotic process dating from that time. Other ex-colleagues regarded that time as being when he went mad although his daughter Eva saw it as a time he found himself. Sharaf (1983) writing of this time in Reich's life states: 'There is not doubt that at Davros [Sanatorium] Reich was taking himself more seriously than ever. From that time on, he saw himself as living or wanting to live a heroic destiny' (p. 120).

Whatever view one takes on this period in Reich's life, from that time on his most creative period occurred. He clearly believed he had found a new truth in his orgone energy, his understanding of the theory of life energy and its flow and pulsation in our bodies and in the universe, and his therapy as a treatment based on this energy. This would fit closely with Ellenberger's notion of the outcome of a creative illness. Certainly Reich's therapeutic work is easier to understand within a shamanic or neo-shamanic frame rather than that of a talking cure. It is also worth noting that several United Kingdom Council for Psychotherapy (UKCP) institutes hold Reich's work in high regard and he is a major figure within the humanistic psychology world. (For a good discussion of Reich's illness and of his life and work in general, see Boadella 1973, Sharaf 1983, or West 1988.)

Jung's illness

During 1913–14 when the break with Freud was becoming absolute, Jung became ever more agitated and unbalanced in his mind, to the point where he accused Freud of being the devil. This was part of a general process of mental disintegration which took him to the edge of the abyss.

(McLynn 1996 p. 233)

In his autobiography *Memories, Dreams, Reflections* published posthumously in 1963 Jung discusses vividly this key phase of his life and speaks of:

An incessant stream of fantasies had been released, and I did my best not to lose my head but to find some way to understand these strange things. I stood helpless before an alien world; everything in it seemed difficult and incomprehensible. I was living in a constant state of tension; often I felt as if gigantic blocks of stone were tumbling down upon me. One thunderstorm followed another. My enduring these storms was a question of brute strength.

(1967 pp. 200–201)

Jung used yoga exercise in order to contain the powerful emotions he was feeling but not to shut down the experiences since he very deliberately faced it, 'As soon as I had the feeling that I was myself again, I abandoned this restraint upon the emotions and allowed the images and inner voices to speak afresh' (p. 201). Despite his very real fear of being taken over by the fantasies he was experiencing, Jung felt he had to explore them partially led by the realisation that he could not expect his patients to do such work if he was unwilling to do the same himself.

Indeed this goes further for as Jung says: 'It is of course, ironic that I, a psychiatrist, should at almost every step of my experiment have run into the same psychic material which is the stuff of psychosis and is found in the insane' (p. 213). The difference was that Jung was not wholly overwhelmed by this often disturbing material and wrestled with it until its meaning became clear. In this process Jung fully developed his theory and practice of analytic psychology and regarded all of his creative work over the next 40 or so years as stemming from that period of working with his fantasies and dreams.

Jung himself recognised that he was close to madness at this point in his life and many 'experts' have produced various diagnoses including schizophrenia (McLynn 1996). This then becomes a convenient basis on which to reject all of Jung's work after his split with Freud. However, Jung's wrestling with his demons can be seen as giving him a deeper insight and experience of his clients' troubles. It is noticeable how a similar stance is taken by the critics of Wilhelm Reich in questioning his sanity. Indeed Reich's favourite-son status with Freud in many ways echoed that of Jung. Such remarks have also been made with regard to Carl Rogers between those who emphasise his Chicago days and regard his work in California as suspect (see under 'Rogers' initiation?').

Ellenberger regards Jung as having a creative illness during 1913–1919 and as having similar features to that of Freud's, namely an 'intense preoccupation with the mysteries of the human soul'. Both had to withdraw from much of their professional lives, both suffered emotional illness and choose self-imposed psychic exercises, and both felt very isolated.

Horney's depression (the dull pain which paralyses the wings of the soul)

Horney was the first, and perhaps the best critic of Freud's ideas about women.

(Quinn 1987 p. 14)

Horney wrestled with Christianity as a young girl brought up in a Lutheran household in the 1890s in Hamburg in Germany. She deeply wanted to experience spirituality and wrote in her diary aged 13, 'In spiritual matters I feel *very unworthy*, for although I am steadily growing up, I do not feel the true need for religion. A sermon can overwhelm me and at times I can act accordingly, but prayer...spiritual poverty – in a word' (quoted in Quinn 1987 p. 30). Horney 'never overcame her religious doubt or gave up her longing for a faith transcending reason' (Quinn 1987 p. 34) but the focus of her searching shifted from religion to study and eventually to psychoanalysis.

Horney's life and work are well worthy of a study, including her ground breaking essay 'The flight from Womanhood' and the way she was forced out of the New York Psychoanalytic Society, whose education committee in 1941 said that her work was resulting in 'preliminary indoctrination with theoretical and emotional orientations which are contrary to the fundamental principles of psychoanalytic education' (quoted in Quinn 1987 p. 14). In the context of this chapter, however, the focus is on in what way her depression might be seen as a creative illness.

She writes to her future husband Oskar in 1906, 'I have so often thought of writing you...Probably that fear again of giving too much, of spiritual undressing – or perhaps because I have a dull suspicion that I could hardly manage to clothe in words what is oppressing me...I have everything, everything, haven't I, that a person could ask in order to be happy – satisfying work, love, home, natural surrounding etc' (Quinn 1987 p. 118).

Later, now married to Oskar, seven months pregnant and working hard on her studies, she writes of experiencing a great exhaustion and 'a longing for sleep – even for death'. She had 'spasms of sobbing', stomach pains, a tightness in her throat and her heart would pound. Soon she sought analysis from Karl Abraham to relieve the 'dull pain which paralyses the wings of my soul' (Quinn 1987 p. 157). The limitations of her analysis by Abraham was lessened by her own self-analysis and her eventual conviction that 'Life itself is the most effective help for our development' (Horney 1942 p. 8).

Horney's desire not to be average 'There is nothing more unbearable than the thought of disappearing quietly in the great mass of the average' (Quinn 1987 p. 156), her drive for intellectual understanding and her inability to accept that which she did not experience as true perhaps made her conflict with the largely male

New York Freudians inevitable. Like her male counterparts Reich and Jung her therapeutic innovations (in her case a challenge to Freud's view of women, a therapeutic valuing of the 'here and now', etc.) led her to perhaps an inevitable and painful split. Unlike Reich and Jung, her split did not produce some kind of breakdown or apparent 'creative illness', in fact she characteristically threw herself into work and almost immediately launched a rival organisation, the Association for the Advancement of Psychoanalysis.

Rogers' initiation?

Is there a case to be made Carl Rogers had a creative illness? Certainly there are two episodes in his life worthy of further exploration. First, his trip to China as a divinity student which led him to abandon theology in favour of psychology and which also resulted in his being hospitalised with a duodenal ulcer and several weeks of subsequent convalescence (discussed in Thorne 1992). Clearly the experience of being in China for 6 months gave Rogers the opportunity to break away from the somewaht rigid Christian life led by his parents. There is a real flavour of Eastern philosophy in client-centred therapy which points to Rogers soaking up more of a Chinese influence than that has been acknowledged. The focus on process and listening seems to me close to the qualities of Daosim with its emphasis on the Way and on flexibility and on light use of authority. Some have seen influences of Zen Buddhism in client-centred therapy. Such influences are more readily acknowledged in Gestalt therapy.

There is another intriguing incident later in Rogers' life in which he took on a very troubled woman for counselling and at some point, he mysteriously left Chicago for a period of time and when he returned he went into therapy for the first time. Clearly something very disturbing had arisen for Rogers during the course of counselling this troubled woman. Thorne (1992) speaks of the two years 'period of great personal distress...[which] threatened to undermine him completely...He emerged from this dark period able to accept himself and to give and receive love in a way which had not previously been possible' (1992 p. 14). Thorne comments that perhaps Rogers was led to create client-centred therapy because he so badly needed the healing it offered himself.

There is a reluctance in the person-centred world to talk about these experiences which might cast Rogers in a more imperfect and human light but also from the viewpoint I am exploring here they point to the possibility of Rogers as a shamanic figure following on from a creative or initiatory illness. (Incidentally in the video of Rogers with Gloria he looks to me very much like a Buddhist monk complete with that beam of peace and well-being that such monks seem to emanate.)

Even if Rogers did not have an intense creative illness his description of his concept of presence has all the flavour of shamanic practice even though it does lack explicit mention of soul retrieval or journeying into the realms of the spirit world on behalf of the client:

> I find that when I am closer to my inner, intuitive self, when I am somehow in touch with the unknown in me, when perhaps I am in a slightly altered state of consciousness in the relationship, then whatever I do seems to be full of healing. Then simply my *presence* is releasing and helpful...I may behave in strange and impulsive ways in the relationship, ways which I cannot justify rationally, which have nothing to do with my thought processes...At these moments it seems that my inner spirit has reached out and touch the inner spirit of the other...Profound and healing energies are present.
>
> (Kirschenbaum and Henderson 1990a p. 137)

The implications of this approach of Rogers have been well explored in a recent book by Brian Thorne (2002) who argues that person-centred therapists can take on the role of being both secular priests and prophets. He argues that such therapists need to adopt a spiritual discipline in order to be able to work with transcendence and the energies involved. I find much to agree with in this stance of Thorne' though it remains deeply controversial within the person-centred world. I return to a discussion of presence in Chapter 4 in the context of making sense of the territory.

Ellenberger (1970) is clear that not every therapist has a creative or initiatory illness. He distinguishes between those who have made a study of their own neurosis from those whose life work stems from their creative illness. From this point of view I reckon Reich, Jung and Freud had creative illnesses but Horney and Rogers probably not. Ellenberger also tells us how Freudian clients produce Freudian dreams and Oedipal conflicts whilst Jungian clients have archetypal dreams and discover their animas!

Cushman (1995) would probably advise us against pursuing this notion of Ellenberger's that Freud and Jung be considered as shaman. He insists that 'therapists are not shamans; shamans are shamans' (p. 3). He further suggests that each era has a particular construction of the self with characteristic illnesses, healers and healing methods, insisting that each is unique and local and not reducible to a universal law. He states: 'nothing has cured the human race, and nothing is about to. Mental ills don't work that way; they are not universal, they are local. Every era has a particular configuration of self, illness, healer technology; they are a kind of cultural package' (p. 7).

My researches

During 1993–1994 I interviewed 30 people whose work as counsellors or psychotherapists in some way included healing. This covered people experiencing special moments in their work which they might talk of in terms of Buber's I/Thou relating (1970) or in terms of Rogers' (1980) concept of presence but it also included people who actively used healing techniques or people who used both. Eight of these people suffered some illness as part of their transition towards healing and three of these seem to fit Ellenberger's description of a creative illness, whilst the other five had less serious but still significant illnesses. Indeed one felt that all the serious illnesses in his life had had a bearing on his development as a therapist. (It is interesting to note that many of the people who took part in my research were female, including six out of the eight who had significant illnesses.)

As we learnt from a consideration of Jung's and Freud's experiences, creative or initiatory illnesses often last for a number of years. One person interviewed showed this and other features of such an illness. She had a breakdown followed by a divorce, got very depressed, attempted suicide and then developed bulimia. Taking part in analytic group therapy for two years helped for a while, but then her depression returned. To add to her suffering she then took a bad fall: 'this chap careered into the back of me...Because I was rolling forward, my legs came up in front of me and I fell and cracked the base of my spine. And it was really traumatic; I couldn't walk. You know how you bang your knee and you think the pain will go off? Well it didn't.'

In retrospect she saw herself as being at that time: 'generally being very lost in my life. I didn't have a direction. I'd lost any sort of spirituality...I'd become very disillusioned and embittered, a lost soul really.' Still suffering from chronic lower back pain she signed up for an academic course. Someone on the course suggested she see a healer, which had a powerful effect on her both physically and psychologically. She reported experiencing: 'all these streams of movement and energy I feel moving in my body; and he wasn't even touching me. And I thought "What the hell is going on?" And I had this feeling, like so many healers, that I'd come home...and I was totally fascinated by the experience of having healing, even though on one level I thought, "Oh well, nothing's happening here." But I also knew on some level that something really important was happening; and that I'd found something that I was meant to get involved with.' This battle to accept the healing experience coupled with a sense of coming home is a familiar reaction for people real-ising that they have a gift for healing.

Another person I interviewed had been suffering from depression, feeling 'for reasons which seem a bit silly now, that I'd wasted my life'. However, he then had a paranormal experience that was to be a turning point in his life. It involved an out-of-body experience and an encounter with a UFO at a spiritual site in Egypt, during which he heard a voice that had 'a sport of silvery, metallic, non-human quality about it'. This voice told him things that made a lot of sense to him, in particular that he had paid a debt and was now guiltless and free. Then a healing occurred 'I felt myself immersed in water, like a healing water, I ceased to feel the sort of psychic pain, guilt and anguish and so on'. Later, back at his hotel he cried for about two hours and felt as if he was completely reborn. On his return to Britain he found that he had the ability to heal.

Another person I interviewed reported being laid low by a mysterious illness: 'I came into healing because I'd had a terrible bad flu which left me having fits in my sleep at night for about six months. I was confused, no concentration, very tired like ME [Myalgic Encephalomyelitis].' Someone suggested she try a course in Silva Mind Control (a form of guided meditation) that is supposed to help memory disturbances, and through contact with people on this course she was led to learn healing.

Mid-life crisis can act as the focus for such a transition. For one woman I interviewed it involved a desire to 'change direction. I didn't know what I wanted to do, but wanting to be more involved with people. I just couldn't be doing with the business world anymore.' A colleague was dying of cancer and sought the help of a healer.

The healing seemed to help even though her colleague died. Later she asked for the name of the healer so that she could get advice. Through talking with the healer she realised she wanted to learn to heal.

The death of individuals close to us can often be the harbinger of change, causing us to question what we are doing with our lives, and sometimes leading to an interest in the spiritual and in healing. So it is perhaps no surprise to learn that bereavement played a key part in the transition of four of the people I interviewed. Indeed, one used her new-found healing skills to: 'more or less assist at my father's death. He was assuaged by whatever I was able to transmit to him. His pain was taken way and so on. But after that I just went completely flat.'

Another woman spoke movingly of the death of her father, and reported that it triggered a state within which she had hallucinations: 'I thought of it as a nervous breakdown, after that I gave up teaching. It was after that that I finished the relationship, it was like everything stopped at that point. It was like a death...got into therapy...I swam around for about 5 years not knowing what I was going to do...and then I became a therapist.'

Another woman interviewed linked her emergence as a healer with the death of both of her parents. The death of her mother from cancer had a huge impact on her: 'one month it (her death) took. And, as you know, anything like that just knocks you for six, and it just makes you look at what the heck is all this about...I'm not happy doing what I am doing, and I started to think, "Why have I been doing this?" I just knew that there was something deeper than what I was doing, and I needed to find it and didn't know how.' Her father's death left her financially secure, which was important to her as a single parent, and thus she was able to pursue her interests in counselling and spiritual healing.

Similarly another woman remarked: 'maybe it was grieving that brought me into healing. I lost my husband and within a year my daughter through suicide. I was so proud that I could cope with my husband – "I'm alright, I can cope" – but of course I was grieving. And when my daughter died as well I was literally brought to my knees mentally and physically and emotionally, as I have never in my life thought I could be, which I needed. I needed a sledgehammer; you know, "Take that!".'

For one woman it was facing herself as she really was, which involved dealing with suicidal thoughts, that was part of her transition. This became in effect a time of death and rebirth for her: 'I was walking down a street in a very old part of town and I suddenly saw myself as I really was, and it was frightening. I saw myself and I didn't like what I saw. And it was the point that I could have killed myself... but simultaneously, a voice came through and said, "I love you in spite of yourself". And it was my own inner voice that had been working just gently, trying to make sense of everything. I'd been to a healing service and I'd met one or two people that I'd felt at peace with, and it was that bit of light that had gone through into me that came up and met the darkness. And at that point I transcended into a place which was absolutely without fear. I knew there was nothing more for me to fear about death, because I had died, I died into myself, and I had been resurrected. And I knew then that there was no fear about dying, because I'd done it. What I had to do then was to go and live, and the living was going to be hard for me 'cos of a lot of unfinished business, with my father who was dead, my mother who was still alive, my sister, my marriage which was not good. I had to resolve that'. Interestingly enough this interviewee, like many of the others mentioned above, does a lot of work with people who are dying or their friends and relatives.

My own transition from therapist to therapist-healer took place during the spring of 1982 (West 1985) in which I opened up to healing and to the psychic realm with great reluctance. I was mindful of Wilhelm Reich's (1952) telling critique of mysticism as being a distorted grasp of life energy based upon not acknowledging its place within oneself, especially its sexual aspect. It was only later I realised how much Reich in his final years had become more spiritual, more accepting of these matters.

I was then having a number of psychic experiences, not especially powerful, but disturbing in themselves which included vivid dreams before and after the death of my aunty, seeing colours, that is, auras around people, seeing faces on occasion in people's auras, hearing imaginary animals and voices. I recognised that these were classic schizoid symptoms, that is, I was seeing and hearing things that most other people would deny existed.

Luckily I sought and received help. I was advised to begin meditation and to be accepting of the experiences that were happening to me. That had a very grounding effect on me that dissipated a lot of the fear involved. A period of real work followed as I came to terms with this new aspect of myself. This involved facing a lot of fear, a lot of crying, becoming more compassionate and less emotionally involved with people's troubles. Gradually there was also a spiritual shift, a deepening of my awareness of my place in the order of things, a spiritual quest that led me to continue my exploration of heretical Christianity and eastern ideas of karma and reincarnation.

All this challenged my deeply held and sometimes rigid humanistic therapeutic view of things. I thought at one point that I would cease to be a therapist and would practice instead as a Spiritual Healer. Later it occurred to me that I could perhaps be both but separately. My attempts to explore their integration led me eventually to do my PhD research study into therapy and healing. I was able to discover links between therapy and spiritual healing including how often similar or same phenomenon are described in different words. For example, much intuitive therapy insight is called clairvoyance by healing.

There was a deep learning for me at that time which is that if I am not doing enough of what I am meant to do however difficult, however impossible it might seem to me, then a process will be set off inside and around me that will encourage me forward whether I like it or not. Such a push comes from the soul level and I believe it cannot be successfully resisted. However much it challenges my lack of self esteem and fear of what others might think including my being seen as foolish, something will feel not right and I will ail until I am sufficiently back on track. That is, Soul or Spirit nudges me and I either listen or the nudges get louder and louder.

Further transitions

As we have seen, the transition to healing can be dramatic and it is by no means the end of the story of change for the practitioner involved. However, it does usually seem to mark a point at which the practitioner is able to accept the role of healer. This is why many of the 30 people I interviewed were willing to work under the label of 'healer', although this was not true in every case. Becoming a healer is no guarantee of good health, or the end of the process of spiritual emergence; further transitions are possible. One woman was clearly going through a deep transition at the time of her interview: 'I'm being stripped of things I have relied on, spiritually stripped. So I had to start all over again with absolutely nothing and it felt like death. And now I'm feeling I have to drop everything, like everything that I'm working in, that has to go too; just being stripped.'

She was moved to describe her experiences in shamanic terms: 'It feels like death of everything that I am, everything I've ever believed, like a shaman's death if you want to put it into grandiose terms. I had it thrust upon me whether I liked it or not.'

For one person interviewed, the further transition had a quality both of what seemed liked burn-out and of the emergence of new approach in her work:

> This winter I'd realised I'd got to do something for myself or I'd almost feel like I won't survive. I've several times got to a place where I've felt that my life energy was just so low it felt like dying. So I'd been forced into this place of change, and so now I am deliberately letting go; clients have fallen away in droves, the workshops I had to run, I've had to give up completely 'cos I was unable to go. It just felt like I cannot support anyone else anymore. I've just got to help myself. My body felt so dried up and empty and my spirit didn't seem able to stay. It's been locked out. I'm not in my body. I'm out there somewhere.

Fortunately three months after this low point, this moment of change and transition, she was able to report that she really felt healed.

For myself doing this research in therapy and healing had felt like a process of initiation itself not just into the world of academia but something much much bigger, I wrote in my research diary at the time: 'What I realize is that doing this study is having a deeper spiritual impact on me than I expected. I am being changed, being initiated.' I felt that this initiation was part of a process of personal and career change, which had been going on for some time and included what I saw as a spiritual aspect. Polanyi points out that such new, heuristic knowing can permanently change us: 'Having made a discovery, I shall never see the world again as before. My eyes have become different; I have made myself into a person seeing and thinking differently. I have crossed a gap, the heuristic gap, which lies between problem and discovery.' (1962 p. 143)

There had also been a further transition for me prior to commencing this research discussed here. Throughout the 1980s into the early 1990s I had regularly co-facilitated five- or seven-day residential therapy groups which proved to be very powerful, very cathartic and life changing for many of the participants. I began to feel trapped by the expectation people had of what doing a group with me would be like. At one group I did a subtle but powerful piece of work with one man which most of the group could not see the point of even though he did.

The next group I co-facilitated I lost my voice half way through. This was to me a (spiritual) sign that I had to cease to run such groups. I stopped organising the groups and therapy centres and groups of people stopped asking me to run or facilitate such groups. It felt like a loss, and was a loss financially as half my income came from such groups but I had no choice but to cease to run them. I was forced to trust in my own spiritual process. Fortunately soon after this I embarked on my PhD studies which at least gave me a framework to hang onto whilst coming to terms with this latest change in my life.

This chapter illustrates how the development of modern psychotherapy has mirrored previous forms of therapeutic care by the therapists involved engaging in their own madness or creative illness. Indeed Ellenberger regarded training analysis undertaken by would-be psychoanalysts as them having their own experience of Freud's illness. Soul attending, a truly holistic approach to psychotherapy requires an ability by the practitioner of being unafraid to engage in these deep levels of human experience, guided in many ways by a knowledge of her or his own deep journeying however painfully acquired.

Chapter 3

The Personal Encounter with Spirituality

Every stage of psychological growth is a step closer to God.
(Wilber 1980 p. 100)

The very feeling which has seemed to me most private, most personal, and hence most incomprehensible by others, has turned out to be an expression for which there is a resonance in many other people.
(Rogers in Kirschenbaum and Henderson 1990a p. 27)

This chapter begins with a consideration of the phenomenological challenge of bracketing before exploring aspects of the spiritual and therapeutic journey that can illuminate spirituality and therapy, using examples drawn from other people's stories and my own experiences and research findings. I then briefly explore spirituality and work before considering others aspects of the spiritual journey including grace and the dark night of the soul.

In attempting to be present to my clients' spirituality I am often reminded of the phenomenological challenge to bracket one's own experience as a therapist or researcher but also of Heron's (1992) memorable statement that total bracketing is impossible. There has been much discussion in the therapy world about the values and ethics that underpin our work (e.g. Richards and Bergin 1997, Bond 2000, West 2002a), and the BACP (2001) new ethical framework for good practice. Clearly therapy is not a value-free activity.

Indeed one of the key fundamental and separating factors between the main schools of therapy is that of the value system underpinning their view of humanity and the therapeutic encounter. For example, consider the striving for authenticity that characterises the existential and humanistic approaches compared with the more cautious, working with transference and counter transference in the psychodynamic and psychoanalytic schools.

When one considers a therapeutic approach that is inclusive of the clients' (and of their therapist's) spirituality, bracketing breaks down in several fundamental ways:

1   Whether one considers spirituality to be potentially healthy or not – at best a 'crooked cure' or a fundamental aspect of human existence.
2   If one is inclusive of healthy spirituality how is this contained within a psychological theory, indeed does counselling and psychotherapy have to be based on psychological theory at all? (e.g. philosophical counselling (Howard 2000) or narrative approaches to therapy (McLeod 1997)).
3   There are phenomena that occur fairly frequently within the therapy session that both client and therapist are likely to label 'spiritual' (Rogers 1980, Buber 1970, West 2000a, Thorne 1991, 1998, 2002).
4   If the client feels that their spirituality and spiritual experiences are acceptable to their therapist, then they will likely explore some aspect of their spirituality within their therapy. Any therapist whose clients never mention spirituality has to ask themselves what their counter-transference issues around spirituality are (Lannert 1991).
5   How we as therapists react to our clients' material and our choices of what we encourage them to focus on and explore is influenced by our own interests, biases and unconscious processes. For example, how often have I heard it said and indeed experienced it myself that my clients this week were all seemingly working on an issue that was very real and pertinent to me. So the spiritually minded therapist will find her or his clients often working on spiritual issues in their therapy.
6   What is really apparent here is that one therapist is not equivalent to another. Perhaps all roads lead to Rome, that is, any competent therapist should be able to help a whole range of people with a variety of problems but the journey they experience itself will be very different. This brings to mind the recent randomised controlled trial done by King (Ward *et al.* 2000) who found that person-centred counselling, Cognitive-Behavioural therapy and usual General Practitioner (GP) care were equally useful to clients suffering from anxiety and depression but that the counselling and therapy clients got better quicker and that those who received the

person-centred therapy particularly enjoyed its approach. The journeying then is important as well as the actual destination.

As a caveat here I will restate that I am not speaking of religion but of spirituality. Counselling within a religious framework puts us into a different frame that will be explored later.

I have elsewhere argued (West 1995a, 2000a) that the regular practice of being a therapist in itself constitutes a form of spiritual practice. For example, being attentive to one's clients whilst being aware of oneself, one's inner processes and doing this for hours at a time, week in week out, over a number of years is unwittingly doing or rather being something akin to what Buddhists' call mindfulness (Tart and Deikman 1991). One would then expect that therapists who practice over 5, 10, 15 or more years would show such a development. I do not yet have the empirical quantitative data on this but only an awareness that many of my colleagues from way back have either gone increasingly psychodynamic or spiritual/transpersonal or both! Of course they may be merely(!) following Jung's oft quoted dictum that the second half of one's life is more concerned with spiritual matters. What data I do have comes from my own qualitative researches and from my own experience.

Spiritual experiences

It feels useful at this point to sketch in some elements of my own spirituality and spiritual journeying, especially in relationship to my development as a therapist, mixed in with examples from my researches and others experiences. Hopefully the sharing of my own experiences is not merely egotism, and indeed they are not as grand or as scary as some, but to indicate both how ordinary such experiences are but also how much they can change who we are and how we live and work.

I am aware that my way of framing, understanding and contextualising these experiences reflects my early Christian upbringing, my New Age and heretical Christian exploring in my 20s and 30s and my more recent membership of the Religious Society of Friends. The value is that these are experiences which I take to be spiritual and are not untypical of what many experience as David Hay would have us believe (Hay and Morisy 1978, Hay 1982, Hay and Hunt 2000).

It so happened that a couple of years ago I was invited to write about my spiritual experiences (West 2000e) and it proved much more difficult for me than I had imagined. Although I had had such experiences on a regular but occasional basis, all of my adult life I felt a curious reluctance to claim them and name them as 'spiritual'. It was one thing to privately hold them dear, another to speak about them. Then I was in York Minster and had the experience described in the introduction on route to a meeting of the Northern Counselling Tutors' Forum. It was therefore timely to own this part of my life and being.

The spiritual experience I had in York Minster included:

1   feeling a sense of being in a spiritual place, if you like I was awestruck;
2   being overwhelmed by the feel of the spiritual energy present in the chapel set aside for prayer and being moved to weep;
3   feeling such a sense of gratitude at being able to feel this (spiritual) energy;
4   a sense of being enabled to return to my true nature or spiritual self. This was immediately followed by a feeling of regret at not living enough from that true centre of mine;
5   spending some time in prayer for those close to me especially those in difficulties;
6   also spending time in contemplation;
7   leaving the Minster feeling uplifted and cleansed and somewhat washed out.

This was yet another spiritual experience for me of a kind that occurs relatively frequently during Quaker Meetings for Worship, visiting churches and other holy sites which include stone circles like Stonehenge and Avebury. Such experiences can occur during quiet moments alone in prayer, meditation or contemplation. Sometimes I have a strong sense during such experiences that changes are occurring in my energy field or aura, and sometimes to the energy field of the Meeting. With my eyes closed or sometimes open I 'see' amethyst coloured light that swirls around the front of my face. This might seem a strange phenomenon but others have reported the same (e.g. Summers 1997). The sense of a return to my own true nature during such spiritual experiences is a regular feature of such events for me.

What strikes me also as significant about this experience is that it occurred on route to a meeting of counselling colleagues. There was a real parallel between my development as a counsellor on my

MA in Keele University and developments in my spiritual and religious life, which was a reflection of similar shifts in my life when I first became a therapist ten years previously. It is as if any new development in my working life, or life as a whole is reflected in and related to developments in my spiritual life. They feed into each other, not always in an easy way.

One of the therapists, let us call him Richard, I interviewed during my research into therapy and healing had a spiritual experience that seemed to have arisen in response to questions in his mind following the death of one of his partner's parents:

> We had a supervision group one where this subject came up of clients who'd been visited by ghosts. And later that day...I'd had a couple of brandies and I was in a very smooth sort of relaxed state, I was sitting reflecting on the pains of my own life, and wondering about what the sense was in it, and sensing there was some sort of ultimate good through my pains and sufferings. And the feeling [of a presence] got stronger and stronger, and in the archway, a sort of tangible presence was manifesting. I couldn't see it, it felt like a male presence and It grew stronger and stronger. And I was asking it questions about my sufferings, and this message was spoken that all would be well, and I started to question it about individual trouble spot, and [was told] all would be well and the terrible sufferings of people in the world had some sort of sense.

There are various ways one could interpret this experience not least noting the consumption of two brandies and one could begin to think about projection and so on. This misses the point of how Richard understood his experience:

> It was a very powerful experience, like one of those biblical ones. I was flooded with tears and my body was absolutely trembling. And on one level I wanted to stay with it for ever, and at the same time it was too much, too much to bear this incredible sense of well-being. And I was at the same time asking this presence to go and to stay, eventually he started to wane and eventually I felt very calm and quite tired. And in the next couple of days after that I was very depressed. It was one of those experiences that really changed my life. I'd been very earthbound before and it really changed my dimensions.

Just over ten years ago as my mother lay dying I felt compelled to attend the nearest Quaker Meeting in Bewdley one of those 1690 meeting houses that I love so much. I found myself in a deep silence and laid down the burden of my mother's dying and in the silence coming to myself I found the final words I needed to say to my mother. I returned to the hospital to find that my mother had briefly spoken out of her coma and asked for me. The words were said – mostly telling her it was OK to let go – and she died an hour or so later. Although I still miss her dearly I am surprisingly at peace in terms of my feelings about her and her death, partially thanks to my spiritual experience at Bewdley that Sunday.

This spiritual experience in relation to death and dying reflects how for many people either dying themselves or being present to others dying has much of the spiritual present in it (see Kubler-Ross 1997, Levine 2000) despite or perhaps sometimes because of the grief and anger that is also often present. It seems as if the confrontation with death is often a trigger for spiritual experiences and spiritual development. Bereavement was a key factor for the transition from therapist to therapist-healer for a number of my respondents in my research into therapy and healing discussed in the last chapter.

Some 30 years ago fresh down from university I was in the countryside near where I lived with a good friend of mine sitting on some sandstone rocks in the sunshine feeling relaxed and a bit meditative and a voice came into my head and said 'love is the essence of being'. This phrase ran around and around inside my head. I did not really know what it meant and contemplated those words for a long time. This was a strange experience that I pondered on for years and which seems now an obvious statement to me if somewhat naïve. It has some echoes of the experience of 'Phyllis' described below in which biblical words come to her. Indeed one of the people I interviewed in my research into therapy and healing, let us call him Alan, spoke of his experience whilst visiting a Saxon Church:

> We got there at dusk and I couldn't find a light switch and we were feeling our way around the walls of this old church. And I felt under what must have been a little tower end, and this voice said, "You have to honour what people have respected in these places", which was quite a heavy message. And I then went to sit besides my partner. And I saw this vision of a country

church and a marriage and flowers and a wedding taking place, and I came out there and then and said, "I think we've got to get married."

Alan commented how he was told what to do at certain times and how it is unambiguous and yes, they did have a marriage in a country church soon afterwards. Alan also described an experience that occurred to him at a stone circle: 'And suddenly I just really had this strong impulse: I knew I had to breakaway from her [his companion] and go and lie down on this flat stone that was lying on the ground. And as I did that I just had this experience of melting, so that I am the stone and the stone going in front of me and the distant sea suddenly were all one. Describing this afterwards I had to put them in sequence, though in that second we were one. And that was because I was told to lie down on this stone and I did it; I just did what I was told.'

More than 30 years ago at the break-up of a teenage romance and feeling like hell for 6 weeks cut off living in an isolated bed sitter, walking in the park and suddenly overcome by the colours, the energy, the life of a peach tree in blossom. My spirit responded as it often did to the beauty of nature. I was lifted out of my personal hell. I take this as a Wordsworth type example of nature teaching me, of me being given a brief sublime moment of transcendence that put my mourning into a context. It took me time to dig myself out of my personal hell at that time and stay out, but help from the Spirit was available to me and has remained ever since. A somewhat similar experience occurred to another of the people I interviewed (call him Clive) around therapy and healing:

I was sitting in the garden one afternoon and looking at something or other on one of the caravans and thinking how ugly it was and how nature puts out a different type of extension, and looking at the beech tree or birch tree alongside. And there was this thought, "I think about where every leaf falls" and I thought "who is I?" And I allowed the thought process to continue, it was to do with planning and the incredible detailed planning of where every leaf falls, and that is part of the plan.

Interestingly Clive does not use the word 'God' but his mention of a plan implies a clear spiritual perspective of the whole of life which he is able to glimpse and experience in that moment.

One occasion in a Quaker meeting, about eight years ago, I picked up the bible to open it at random and read something about stoning adulterers and something that could be read as against homosexual relationships. I felt disturbed by these words and a feeling arose in me that I would probably have to stand up and speak about this, but meanwhile something else happened to me. In my mind's eye I became a foetus that was poisoned and I was in the centre of the meeting and the black poison was flowing out of me. I was in floods of tears at the relief. (Often in those early days I was in tears, mostly of relief, as I came home to who I truly was.) Then someone else arose and spoke eloquently about having a gay son which relieved me of the need to speak.

This is a vivid example of:

1   The kind of spiritual therapeutic experience that occurred quite commonly for me in those early days of attending Quaker Meetings without having to 'explain' my feeling to a counsellor or therapist, merely to experience the relief, the letting go and the moving on.

2   The fairly common Quaker experience of a kind of synchronicity (Jung 1967) where one person either says what another was about to say (and bear in mind that Quaker meetings are mostly held in silence with a few brief spoken contributions from time to time out of the silence) or where one speaks about something that is deeply troubling that person in a healing way.

There have been other less dramatic occasions when meeting with fellow counsellors or with Quakers for various purposes, or on retreat, when I have felt so spiritually close to the other people present that I have felt transformed. I have discussed and described these experiences as 'spiritual spaces' (West 1995a, 1997, 1999, 2000a). Of course it does not always happen and it certainly is not predictable. I have learnt to realise that it is a gift, if you are happy with the word it is Grace, and it happens when it happens. Thankfully when I am very low it can happen or I have at times been very restless when it has occurred.

Of course not all spiritual experiences feel wholly positive or free from fear, and play a potentially useful role for therapy. Looking at spiritual experiences within the psychotherapeutic frame Maslow (1970) put forward the notion of 'peak experience' which Wilber (1979b) usefully referred to as 'peek' experience and Anthony *et al.* (1987) talk of glimpses. The notion is that we sometimes have these glimpses of a more developed sense of ourself as a spiritual being. Unfortunately, we are unable to remain at that state of consciousness. However, such a peak experience can leave us permanently changed. As we progress on our spiritual journeys, the quality of our spiritual or peak experiences can change, Wilber's spectrum of consciousness model can be helpful here and will be explored in the next chapter.

Spirituality and work

Of course spiritual experiences can arise out of one's work and in Chapter 5 I explore examples of how the therapy session itself can have moments that feel special or spiritual. However, there are other, perhaps less direct, ways in which the ordinary encounters at work can have a spiritual quality.

One of the Quakers I interviewed about her work (West 1998a), let us call her Phyllis, described an incident from a time before she was a Quaker when she had more or less rejected her Anglican upbringing and described herself as agnostic:

At one stage in my career I was a hospital social worker and one of my duties was to cover accident and emergency. And I went in early one very cold day and I was called to accident and emergency, and the sister said to me, "Put your overall on, we've got a filthy tramp". And it was her tone of voice in rejecting this man, sort of got at me, and I went across and they'd put this man in a corner, really the leper, and they said, "Get him out of here, we've already had to take one ambulance out of service, fumigate it, we just want him out, there's nothing physically wrong with him."

So, I went across to talk to him and he was sort of beyond hope really, and they said that he'd been found in Richmond, passed out, he'd collapsed, so I said to him, "When did you last eat?" He just sort of shrugged, and I said, "Well would you like a cup of tea, a cheese sandwich something like that?" ... So I went and found it and as I bent over him I could feel things hopping about in his head and he really was filthy, and instead of being appalled, the words came into my head, "In as much as you have done this for one of mine [you are doing this for me]" I thought where's that coming from?

In this moment of caring for the tramp rather than being disgusted like the nurse was with his filthy condition Phyllis has a compassionate response and finds words from Jesus coming to mind. No doubt these were very familiar words to her stemming from her early Anglican upbringing. She describes its effect on her: 'It was so strong, but it took me a long time to piece all this together...I can't imagine how God was so patient, all that time waiting for him to give me this message and for me to accept it.' Soon afterwards Phyllis attended her first Quaker meeting.

There are of course a number of ways of viewing Phyllis' experience. During an act of compassionate care for the tramp, why should she not remember words from her early Christian upbringing? However, this would be to miss the point. From Phyllis' point of view these words came from outside of her and from God. The impact on her was so profound that she shortly afterwards joined Quakers after 30 years of agnosticism.

It may well prove a challenge to people not familiar with, or accepting of such God language, to see the truth for Phyllis is this experience. During my researches into therapy and healing I sent a brief questionnaire to the 30 people I had interviewed as part of the study to ask them about which healing phenomena occurred in their work. One of the questions I asked was, 'Did they feel that God was present in their work?' Ten of the twenty-seven people who filled in the questionnaire replied 'Yes'. I found this challenging as I was much more comfortable with the notion of special spiritual or healing moments occurring but to maintain that God was present is a whole other matter.

Now, of course, the people I interviewed for my research into therapy and healing were not a typical group and so would be much more likely to reply 'Yes' to such a question than most therapists would. Nevertheless I am beginning to wonder if what goes on privately in the therapy room is pretty different from what is publicly discussed. For example, there is a real question mark over the use of prayer in counselling (e.g. Rose 1993, 1996, Richards and Bergin 1997, West 2000a, Gubi 2001, 2002, 2003). A recent survey by Peter Gubi (2002) BACP of accredited counsellors revealed a surprising number who used prayer in their work. Of the 247 respondents (43 per cent return rate) 12 per cent had used prayer overtly with Christian clients and some 59 per cent had used prayer covertly. Of this later group 37 per cent had prayed for guidance during a session, 25 per cent had prayed for their client during a session, 49 per cent outside of a session, and 51 per cent had used prayer to prepare themselves. Only 24 per cent of those using prayer had discussed it in supervision despite the ongoing debate about whether prayer is an appropriate part of counselling.

Other aspects of the spiritual journey

Of course I do not want to give the impression that the spiritual journey is all about frequent powerful spiritual experiences of the kind described above. For most people these are relatively few and far between. Indeed some would say that the spiritual life is not about such spiritual experiences and spiritual phenomena, and for many people that seems to be true. Indeed some schools of spiritual development advise against becoming too caught up in spiritual phenomena – some of the Buddhist ones for example. Nevertheless it is precisely the power of these experiences that I have described above and how they are frequently linked to mental illness that makes them an appropriate matter for the therapy room.

Such spiritual experiences come when we most need them but they do not come to order and there can be times of aridness of feeling like one is in a spiritual desert without any nourishment. Indeed St John of the Cross, a famous 16th-century mystic coined the phrase, 'dark night of the soul' (Backhouse 1988) to describe the experience of feeling cut off from God. He is clear, however, that this is part of a process of spiritual development.

Besides the drama of the full-blown spiritual or mystical experience there are quieter spiritual moments. From time to time the counselling process or one's life in general seems to be touched by what – to use perhaps a Christian notion – we could call Grace. Grace appears, as a gift, it is not earned, it turns up when it chooses to, often but not always at the time of greatest difficulty, sometimes arriving when things are going well enough only to add to the sense of well-being. Those special and spiritual moments of the therapeutic encounter – discussed elsewhere – which have been called I/Thou relating, or presence, or tenderness can all be seen as Grace.

There is another side to all of this of course. Sometimes the delight of Grace, the joy of being on the spiritual path can collapse like a soufflé and then it can feel like one is in that dark night of the soul:

> God leaves them in complete darkness so that they are not able to use their minds or meditate as they did before, since their inner senses are buried in this night. They are left only with a kind of dryness which not only excludes pleasure and comfort in spiritual exercises which used to give great pleasure, but also gives them insipid and bitter tastes in these matters.
>
> God has seen that they have grown a little and so are strong enough to be weaned and leave off their baby clothes. He puts them down from his arms and teaches them to stand on their own two feet. They feel very wobbly in this strange experience.
>
> (St John of the Cross in Backhouse 1988 p. 24)

We could usefully compare this medieval spiritual diagnosis of the dark night of the soul with our modern secular diagnosis of clinical depression to see in what ways they overlap and to also consider the possible treatment offered. Perhaps in the 21st century we can still learn something from our medieval counterparts who saw themselves involved in the 'care of souls' (Ellenberger 1970).

The 'ordinary' pains and sufferings of everyday life can, I think, trigger something akin to this experience of the dark night of the soul and indeed as with mystical experiences and psychosis the question can arise: Is this a spiritual process or is it a severe depression? And of course the best answer to this kind of question is what will be of most use and most help to the suffering individual involved. Certainly medicating someone out of such a process/ experience is not always the best help to them. Sometimes we have to wrestle with the demons and with the angels to become, para- doxically, more fully human. It is to be hoped that therapists could be one source of support for those of us undergoing such wrestling. The next chapter should provide such therapists with some further light on how to make sense of the psycho- spiritual realm.

In this chapter I have focused largely on dramatic examples of spiritual experiences of the kind that occur to some people. It is worth recalling David Hay's cumulative figure of 76 per cent reporting some kind of spiritual experience. Many of the issues raised by those experiencing this or these phenomena seem to my mind to be appropriate concerns for the therapeutic encounter. The next chapter will focus on how we make sense of this psycho-spiritual territory.

Chapter 4

Making Sense of the Territory

As my contribution to making sense of therapeutic work within a psychospiritual frame, I will sketch in this chapter various models or ways of looking at the territory. These include: Tseng and Hso, Buber, Wilber, Shamanism, Rogers' presence, cultural issues and a model from my research. The final section of this chapter will consider the notion of therapy itself as a faith journey.

There are four key points that I wish to make at the start of this chapter:

1   Our discourse around therapy seems inadequate to me, just not up to the task of discussing what therapy is all about. I am mindful of the fact that many of the early theoreticians of therapy such as Freud, Jung, Klein, Rogers and more were innovative clinicians who then had to develop concepts and a language in which to talk about therapy.

2   Much good therapeutic work probably occurs in an altered state of consciousness for both client and therapist (Wilber 1979a, Thorne 2002). Certainly for many, the experiences connected with spirituality occur not in our ordinary state of mind. Such experiences are not always possible to recall at all or if so the words to describe them may simply not exist (Boucouvalas 1980, Rowan 1983, Vaughan 1989, West 1995a).

3   As mentioned earlier I am struck by how many of my colleagues, and beyond them the more well-known figures within our therapeutic world, who have gone either increasingly psychodynamic/psychoanalytic in orientation as they have got older and more seasoned, or have gone spiritual and possibly transpersonal for whom I coined the aphorism 'Old therapists don't die they just go spiritual.' A few rare brave souls go both psychodynamic and transpersonal more or less simultaneously!

4   I think our understanding of the whole area of therapy and spirituality is increased if we view it within a multi-cultural postmodern context. If we can study and above all accept and value aboriginal forms of healing within the various communities – including our own – then we have a better chance of a fuller more integrated grasp of psychospiritual healing.

I find that trying to fit my ongoing sense of myself as a therapeutic practitioner within some kind of therapeutic frame is a highly challenging process. Even more challenging is trying to talk about the various therapists and writers around therapy and spirituality and to fit them into some kind of model or at least make some kind of sense of it all. Thankfully Ken Wilber has developed one key and important psychospiritual model that will be discussed later. His model has been much debated over the past 20 or so years since he first published it and it is likely to keep spiritually minded therapists in debate and discussion for many years to come!

Tseng and Hso (1979)

This model, see Figure 4.1, has been much used within the therapy world (e.g. Lago and Thompson 1996).

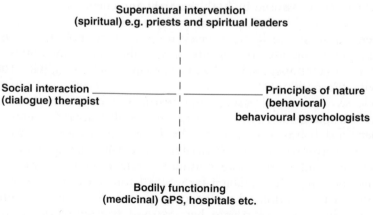

FIGURE 4.1   Four healing methods

Looking at this model I realise how much therapists prefer to occupy the social or interaction (dialogue) part of the diagram with much discourse around therapy as a talking cure. This position is in denial of the more dramatic and also more spiritual roots of modern psychotherapy and counselling. This makes it harder to talk about the territory and leaves our vocabulary for such conversations limited. It also makes the whole thing scarier (see Linda Ankrah's experience of spiritual emergency discussed below under 'Culture') and can involve re-inventing the wheel. The enthusiastic adoption of much of modern therapy by many in the Christian Church and other faiths (despite some notable opposition from Leech (1994) among others) has added to the problem so that the spiritual life has itself become psychologised. It is as if the religious life in Britain dare no longer call itself by its true name. Robinson (1997) spoke of this in terms of 'ontological collapse', and it is one of Rowan's (1993) telling criticisms of Jung – namely that he psychologised the spiritual.

Returning to the model we can see how therapists have been largely pulled towards the medical axis rather than the spiritual, as psychotherapy and especially counselling has grown and developed within the health service. This chapter, and indeed this book is concerned with the territory between social and spiritual intervention. Indeed it can be seen as being a creative place midway between therapy and the spiritual where, without actively seeking supernatural interventions, the spiritual unfolding of the client's therapeutic process has particularly special more 'spiritualised' moments which are recognised by both therapist and client.

I used to think that the maximum possible growth in one's therapeutic practice came from being able to work with, or facilitate extreme states in one's clients. I was attracted to therapies like Reichian therapy (West 1994a,b) which works very powerfully with the body, with breathing and with emotional and physical release. I was also attracted to, or rather compelled towards, spiritual healing and the channelling of powerful healing energies to benefit the client (West 1985, 1995a). Whilst still seeing the point of these approaches I no longer felt that drawn to practising them. Instead I feel drawn to *be* with my clients within a spiritual frame and then, hopefully, their (spiritual) therapeutic process *unfolds*. (Such a focus on being with the client and not doing is also proposed by Geller (2001) in her discussion of presence explored below.) This way of working is probably not as dramatic as the extreme states referred to above but it is seemingly as least as effective. Sometimes in trying to talk about it I feel as if I am trying to hold water in the palm of my hand as it trickles through my fingers. However, my case studies and vignettes in Chapter 5 do convey something of this process of witnessing, of a kind of midwifery to that which is wanting to be psychically born within the client and their world.

Buber's refusal of models

Martin Buber was a Jewish philosopher (1878–1965) who has had a huge impact on the therapy world especially those of a humanistic persuasion including person-centred therapy and Gestalt therapy. Buber (1970) writes movingly and poetically about spirituality in everyday human relating. He suggests that there are two basic ways in which we relate to each other: we either treat each other as object and have an I–It relationship or we treat each other as subject or kin and have an I–Thou relationship. In healthy relating there will be movement between I–Thou and I–It forms of relating.

To Buber the I–Thou relationship was essentially spiritual and God was to be experienced within the inbetween, the connectedness of the two people. As Buber put it: 'There is no I taken in itself, but only the I of the primary word I–Thou and the I of the primary word I–It...If I face a human being as my Thou, and say the primary word I–Thou to him, he is not a thing among things, and does not consist of things' (1970 p. 24).

To Buber there are not degrees of I–Thou so it is not something that can be modelled or taught, only experienced. Talking about it is not the same as experiencing it. To Buber an I–Thou relationship was an equal relationship so it could not apply to a therapy relationship or to a teaching relationship. This has not stopped therapists including Rogers (1980) and more recently Clarkson (1990) claiming that I–Thou occurs in therapeutic encounters. In a famous dialogue with Rogers (Kirschenbaum and Henderson 1990b), Buber takes Rogers to task for claiming equality, and thereby I–Thou was possible within the therapy relationship. Buber's point was that clients come for therapy because they have problems. Therapists may have problems but these are never disclosed nor become the focus of the therapeutic encounter: therefore the encounter can never be equal. Despite this important caveat Buber's I–Thou is a powerful and useful way of viewing those moments when the therapeutic encounter is seemingly spiritually enthused and where there is a sense of timelessness and expansiveness in which the clients' view of their problem can often be transformed. Buber's warning about the impossibility of modelling or measuring I–Thou is also an important caveat to those of us too taken up with models, with maps rather than the territory.

Wilber's model

Ken Wilber (1979b, 1980, 2001a,b) is probably the key transpersonal theoretician to have emerged in the last 20 years. He has even been referred to as the Einstein of the transpersonal and his impact on those who connect with spirituality and therapy seems to justify such a claim. For anyone making a serious study of therapy and spirituality that includes the transpersonal (and staggeringly too many writers still do ignore and exclude the transpersonal) Wilber's model deserves serious consideration. Not everyone welcomed his model – Heron (1992, 1998) is a key British critic, and Washburn (1990) challenges his model in terms of theories of transcendence. Wilber does also have his defenders which include Vaughan (1986), Rowan (1993) and Walsh (Walsh and Vaughan 1994). I have noticed that therapists I know who are Buddhist tend to be most critical of his theories which is somewhat surprising due to Wilber's own exploration of many forms of Buddhism and its influence on his model. Incidentally, one of the telling criticisms of Wilber is that his model is somewhat linear, hierarchical and implicitly male, although the tragic death a few years ago of Wilber's wife had a huge impact on him including the way it challenged his theories (Wilber 2001a).

I include in Table 4.1 a pared down and simplified version I did of Wilber's 10 stage model of human spiritual development that owes a lot to Rowan's (1993) simplification of Wilber's model to four stages. Wilber's model is a model in which each new stage includes the previous one, rather like a Russian doll that gets bigger and bigger as each new doll incorporates all the previous ones. The earlier stages bear some relationship to Freud's model but start pre-birth, however Wilber's model has almost as many stages beyond Freud's notion of maturity and these take us into realms of human development that are increasingly explicitly spiritual. A major contribution of Wilber's model was to suggest not only that there are specific developmental issue for each stage but also

TABLE 4.1 Simplified version of Wilber's model

Wilber level	Persona/shadow	Centaur	Subtle self	Causal self
Rowan position	Mental ego	Real self	Soul	Spirit
Social goal	Socialisation	Liberation	Extending	Salvation
Traditional role of helper	Physician or analyst	Growth facilitator	Advanced guide	Priest(ess), sage
Therapeutic approach	Psychoanalysis, cognitive-behavioural; some transactional analysis	T-groups, Gestalt, open encounter, person-centred; bodywork	Psychosynthesis, some Jungian, transpersonal	Zen, Taoism, Christian mysticism, Sufi, some Judaism, Goddess, mystics

to propose the most likely useful form or forms of therapeutic or spiritual intervention for that stage.

This has implications for the whole outcome debate, for clients come to therapy for problems of differing kinds. For example, a phobia or a problem of lack of self-confidence may well be very different to a bereavement or existential crisis. Wilber and Rowan are suggesting that differing therapies work at differing levels of human spiritual development. Whilst we might disagree about what therapy works with what condition best (and the evidence where available points to the individual therapist and therapeutic alliance as key variables) and whilst we might disagree with aspects of Wilber's model I think it does represent a helpful notion.

The biggest problems with Wilber's model are, first, that there are some underlying spiritual assumptions to it that not everyone agrees with. For example that the ultimate development of humankind is to be at one with everything. Secondly, although there is an innate flexibility in his model it can be, and sometimes is, regarded and taken as a step by step linear hierarchical model that then does a serious disservice to many people's experience of their own spiritual development. For example, those of us who see their spiritual development as being spiral in which we return to a familiar place but experience it from a more developed human and spiritual position, or those of us who move between various states of spiritual consciousness without a clear and linear sense of development. Nevertheless Wilber's achievement in constructing a model that has application and relevance has led to a massive debate and a depth of engagement with this whole area that is to be welcomed.

Shamanism

A shamanic frame or model might prove useful and shamanism was explored in Chapter 2. It is important that we do not get caught up in the drama of the various shamanic healing rituals however engaging. For there is a Western seeking after extreme experiences and quick fixes which gives shamanism an attractiveness and a glamour. This ignores the cultural context within which the shaman works including the period of preparation the shaman's clients go through before their therapeutic encounter with him or her. The shaman's task of either retrieving part of the client's soul that has got lost and/or engaging with beings in the spirit world on behalf of the client is a powerful metaphor, and possibly a spiritual reality of how people's deepest problems seem linked to the word 'soul' and to some damage, fantasised or real at that very level.

There seems such a rich discourse that never quite completely goes out of fashion or gets lost and which feels truly cross-cultural that does involve the word 'soul', and very evocative statements are made by clients and other people just going about their ordinary lives that use this word. Some forms of music are said to have or lack or even to be soul. Certain people and institutions are said to be soulless – powerful criticisms indeed. Some jobs are said to be soul-destroying. Fear is said to eat the soul. 'It touches my soul' is a strong statement of being moved by something. I see these words as powerful metaphors, as forms of spiritual truth-telling that are barely acknowledged for what they are.

If shamanism is cross-cultural then we can look for examples of its practice within our Western societies. The ongoing and surviving undercurrents of traditional healing, fortune-telling and folk medicine even when they are reframed as New Age point us to an enduring and possibly shamanic feature of our society that predates modern therapy and medicine (discussed by Willis 1992a,b) and that has always lived in a state of tension with Christianity. For example, spiritual healing was illegal in Britain until the 1950s under an ancient Witchcraft Act!

Presence and tenderness

Rogers (1980) points us towards the psychospiritual with his concept of presence suggesting that it is a fourth condition to add to what he previously suggested were three necessary and sufficient conditions for therapeutic change to occur for the clients – namely empathy, congruence and positive unconditional regard. Rogers died before the full implications and research into presence could be undertaken. He and his colleagues had already done a lot of innovative research and clinical work with his three core conditions.

It is worth quoting Rogers in some detail here:

> I find that when I am closer to my inner, intuitive self, when I am somehow in touch with the unknown in me, when perhaps I am in a slightly altered state of consciousness in the relationship, then whatever I do seems to be full of healing. Then simply my presence is releasing and helpful ... I may behave in strange and

impulsive ways in the relationship, ways which I cannot justify rationally, which have nothing to do with my thought processes... At these moments it seems that my inner spirit has reached out and touched the spirit of the other...Profound growth and healing energies are present.

(Rogers in Kirschenbaum and Henderson 1990a p. 137)

There has been some discussion, exploration and research into 'presence' since that time. Van Belle (1990) criticised Rogers for not providing clear guidelines for his 'mystical and spiritual' work and says he does not tell us 'what new things a therapist must do to facilitate this mystical transpersonal experience in clients' (1990 p. 54). Mearns (1994) reframes presence within the light of the three core conditions and does not see it as necessitating a spiritual viewpoint. Brian Thorne (1991, 2002) joyfully embraces the spiritual implications of presence, and has linked it into congruence especially. Thorne introduced the word 'tenderness' which seems certainly akin to Roger's presence.

It is difficult to do justice to Thorne's tenderness without quoting him at length. He provides a brief definition which then needs unpacking, namely: 'When tenderness is present in a relationship I believe that there is the possibility of finding wholeness and of recognising the liberating paradox' (1991 p. 77). Thorne recognises that what he is talking about is hard to put into words. He then talks in terms of 'heightened awareness'. He goes on to say: 'I feel in touch with myself to the extent that it is not an effort to think or to know what I am feeling. It is as if energy is flowing through me and I am simply allowing free passage.' (1991 p. 77).

More courageously Thorne then says:

I feel a physical vibrancy and this often has a sexual component and a stirring in the genitals...It seems as if for a space, however brief, two human beings are fully alive because they have given themselves and each other permission to be fully alive. At such a moment I have no hesitation in saying that my client and I are caught up in a stream of love. Within this stream there comes an effortless or intuitive understanding and what is astonishing is how complex this understanding can be. It sometimes seems that I receive my client whole and thereafter possess a knowledge of him or her which does not depend on biographical data.

(Thorne 1991 p. 77)

Thorne warns us of the difficulty in trusting such moments but suggests that if therapist and client can, then the client will benefit greatly. Clearly it is an unbounded space that he is talking about and the potential for clients to remember previous but abusive experience is high. It takes courage to work as a therapist in such a way and Thorne's writing in this area has been controversial to say the least. Good quality supervision is clearly a must.

The clearly spiritual significance of this way of working is acknowledged in the statement, 'there may be an urgent need to talk about death or God or the soul' (1991 p. 77). As perhaps a final statement on the powerful healing implications of this approach Thorne tells us: 'My hunch is that, with some of my clients, it is in a moment of tenderness that I am able to extend to them that welcome to the world which they never received at birth' (1991 p. 79).

Geller (2001, Geller and Greenberg 2002) has pursued the research side of presence in a doctoral study that combined a qualitative study of how experienced practitioners used presence together with a scale for measuring it. She maintains that it is possible to teach it. Her research into presence produces a model divided into three domains:

1   Preparing the ground for presence which includes both the therapist preparation in her or his life (which includes meditation and other forms of self care) and preparation in the session (which includes bracketing and offering the three core conditions).

2   The process of presence which includes receptivity (including bodily receptivity), inwardly attending (self as instrument, authenticity, etc.) and extending and contact (transparency, intuitive responding, etc.).

3   Experiencing presence which includes immersion (absorption, intimacy in the moment, focused, etc.), expansion timelessness, energy and flow, inner spaciousness, enhanced awareness, etc.), grounding (centred and ease) and being with and for the client (intent on the client's healing, love, lack of self-consciousness).

It should be noted that her model was derived from interviewing seven experienced therapists. However the views of clients are explored by her in a further study. She maintains that presence is the necessary foundation and precondition of the relationship conditions which is contrary to those who see it as a flowering of applying the core conditions.

I have explored these models and frameworks in some detail to give us a variety of views of the psychospiritual territory, to open up thought and debate without feeling a need to say this is the best or this is the one I choose. Psychospiritual reality is too vast and complex to be contained within any simple model and there is the ever present danger that we might mistake the map for the territory or in religious terms obedience to the creed taking the place of the lived spiritual life.

These frames are however valuable for the necessary discussion around psychospiritual practice and a vital contribution to effective supervision. Rowan (2001) has written an essential paper on transpersonal supervision that draws on Wilber's model as well as the ten forms of spiritual emergency put forward by Grof and Grof (1986, 1989).

Culture

One factor that is irreversibly bound up with religion and spirituality is that of culture. In discussing culture I have a great sense of being (in that old Biblical phrase) a fool rushing in where angels fear to tread. Nevertheless culture needs exploring (West and McLeod 2003). McLeod (2001b) has suggested that we view counselling (and by extension psychotherapy) as a social rather than a psychological process. Drawing on the social constructionist viewpoint of Gergen (1985, 1996) he maintains that 'counselling represents one of the many ways in which cultural norms and values of a society are affirmed, and operates as a means of helping people to negotiate their own relationship with these cultural norms' (McLeod 2001b p. 589). This puts the counselling and psychotherapy process clearly and explicitly into a cultural frame where I believe it belongs. It is important that as therapists we do acknowledge culture and the part we are playing in it and the part we play in the cultural lives of our clients and the ways in which clients' problems can be contextualised in cultural terms.

Roy Moodley (1998, 1999) has written extensively about the cultural context in which counselling and psychotherapy occurs. Two of his most intriguing case vignettes are about clients who consult traditional healers at the same time as undergoing psychodynamic therapy with him. The first client is a South Asian man who Roy calls Shiva. Roy describes the impact on Shiva of consulting the Vaid – traditional healer: 'through the traditional healer he was able to identify cultural metaphors, symbols and archetypes which may have been outside the parameters of Western counselling and therapy...The process with the Vaid offered him an alternative narrative in interrogate his disturbances and conflicts' (1999 p. 148).

Moodley presents a second vignette of a black woman referred to as Jo-Anne, who consults a local Obeahman (traditional African Caribbean healer). Moodley comments: 'clearly it seems that Jo-Anne was at a stage that necessitated this move from a Western-trained therapist to a traditional black healer' (1998 p. 501). Moodley argues for the importance of the client from an ethnic minority group having the choice of whether to include a traditional healer within their therapy. He suggests that when a client moves from Western counselling to traditional healing then perhaps they engage with a deeper level of their consciousness. In the postmodern world of changing cultures and sub-cultures I would extend this argument to include the same possibilities for all of us. Indeed, many people are now engaged in multiple consultations with medics, therapists and healers around their problems in living. Roy Moodley has also pointed out how many white people in mixed race relationships are now consulting traditional healers from their partner's culture. Roy invites us to consider the challenge faced by counselling over the next decade in acknowledging and including traditional healing methods (Moodley 1999). He further comments, 'a failure to fully comprehend the role of traditional healing may lead to a narrowing of understanding of "race", culture identity and psychopathology in clinical settings' (p. 149). He concludes that by so recognising traditional healing methods the Eurocentric and individualistic discourse of counselling will be challenged and changed. We await this hopeful development.

Linda Ankrah (2000, 2002) has done some fascinating research into counselling and spiritual emergencies. She speaks of her own experience of 'growing up in a multicultural community in England brought me into close personal contact with the beliefs and perceptions about healing held by people of many different cultures. In many cases, no strong boundary was seen between physical, psychological and spiritual aspects of an illness, and experiences of hearing voices or seeing visions were accepted as normal everyday occurrences' (2002 p. 55).

Linda relates how as an adult she went through a time of experiencing strong and extreme emotions, contact with nature and would occasionally hear a voice inside her head which she had dialogue with. However, when she tried to share her experiences with those around her they fell silent and tended to withdraw from her. She comments: 'What had begun as an extraordinary experience began to develop into a "crisis" in which I felt more and more uncomfortable' (2002 p. 55). People seemed afraid of what she was saying; afraid of her so in fear of being pathologised she became silent.

She found comfort and understanding in a study of some Western psychotherapy writers on spirituality including Jung (1963), Rogers (1980) and especially Grof with his concept of spiritual emergency (Grof and Grof 1989). She also gained much from reading about African forms of spirituality and traditional healing from Na'im Akbar (1984, 1994), Wade Nobles (1980) and Amos Wilson (1993).

Linda was led to research this area and 20 ex-therapy clients responded to a largely qualitative questionnaire. All 20 reported at least once 'non-ordinary experience such as visions, hearing voices, and losing contact with the material world. Although none reported their counsellor as being hostile, five indicate they were unhelpful. One said, 'he ... always wanted to interpret experiences in relation to emotional or psychological explanations', another felt that her counsellor was 'generalising in her feedback' (Ankrah 2002 p. 57).

Disturbingly six out of the thirteen European clients found their counsellors helpful whilst only one out of the seven non-European found their counsellor helpful. Eight out of the thirteen European clients got a positive response from their counsellor discussing such experiences compared to only two out of the seven non-European clients. Although we cannot generalise on such a small sample these findings echo other evidence that clients from ethnic minority groups are less likely to be referred to counsellors or psychotherapists and are less likely to have a positive experience, less likely to turn up for their second session than their white counterparts (Lago and Thompson 1996, Sue and Sue 1990).

During her research interviews, Linda made increasing sense of her own spiritual emergence (Ankrah, personal communication 2002). Some of her respondents spoke in terms of Celtic spirituality including a connectedness with nature, especially trees. This mirrored part of Linda's own experience and led her to explore her Irish spiritual roots as she had previously done with her African roots. She suggests that anyone of a mixed race background should consider exploring spiritual traditions from both families in order to become spiritually whole and to make sense of any spiritual emergence that occurs.

In the National Health Service, psychotherapists talk of working only with psychologically minded clients. This might well be an appropriate use of a scarce and expensive resource. However, it is likely that would-be clients from ethnic minority groups are disadvantaged by this concept that has to be considered within its cultural context.

Wayne Richards challenges us not to accept and collude with the illusion of race: 'I suggest that we need to get rid of racial categorisation on the grounds that it operates to protect the status quo' (1999 p. 8). He points out how the increasing use of ethnic minority categories in the Census and other official documentation whilst seeking to gain information to better target resources is based on white and others. Little attempt has been made to further divide the white category, whilst black does get sub-divided. 'On inspection, the current ethnic monitoring categories appear idiosyncratic because they are based upon a mixture of ideological, biological and geographical notions which tend only to confuse concepts of race, ethnicity and culture' (1999 p. 5). Richards is currently researching heuristically the experiences of people living between racial boundaries. Discussing his initial engagement with his research questions he comments: 'I am left with the question: is it possible to achieve authentic relationship with others across racialised boundaries?' (Richards 2001 p. 4).

Richards' work challenges us at a very deep level to consider what 'race' means to us, including the invitation to consider whiteness as not merely not being black or other. There is a religious equivalent of this which is not to think in terms of Christianity and others. It is useful to reflect on how varied the word 'Christian' is. How different a charismatic fundamentalist Christian is from a Christian Quaker. Notice how the new Archbishop of Canterbury was forced to backtrack with regard to ordaining gay priests, his own fundamentalists would not accept it and he had to give in (*The Guardian* 19 November 2002). Also to reflect whether we consider our religion to be superior. In this context notice how the Chief Rabbi was forced to change what he had written (Sacks 2002) because he dared to imply that there was spiritual truth to be found in other faiths. I was struck at the time by how both religious leaders were reined in by the fundamentalist or traditionalist wings of their faiths just at the point when they were courageously beginning to engage with the modern multicultural multifaith world where sexual discrimination is challenged. As Hughes so rightly says: 'The real divisions in the Church today are not divisions between Christian denominations but between those Christians who have opened the treasure and live with the life it provides, and those Christians who are still sitting on closed boxes, alarmed and afraid, and condemning those who show signs of a new life in Christ' (1985 p. 114). In this context the treasure Hughes refers to is the Christ to be found within the self.

Pittu Laungani vividly describes his cultural shock at moving from India to England as a young man. He writes: 'England to me, came as a shock! I was bewildered by the English! There were as many accents there as there are dialects in India – or almost. Each of them as though spoken in a different tongue, and a few even in forked tongues! It was difficult to distinguish between levity and seriousness, between jest and truth, between praise and censure, between affection and affectation, between acceptance and rejection' (2001 pp. 4–5).

He comments on the lack of interest or even curiosity shown in his cultural background and how he felt pushed to give up his own culture, 'I soon began to realise that in order to relate with the English and thus get on in a reasonable but superficial manner with them, it would be *I* who would be expected to make all the adjustments. Not they. In other words, I would have to learn to assimilate into their culture – if I could get round to understanding it' (2001 p. 6).

The net result of his 30 odd years of living in England and engaging with English culture is that: 'When I am in India, I am accused of being too English (whatever that means) and in England, when the English can bring themselves to express an opinion – I am accused of being "too Indian", (whatever *that* might mean). I am thus, in a no-win situation' (Laungani 2001 p. 21). Laungani offers us the metaphor of the turtle whose shell is our cultural heritage, destroy the shell and you destroy the turtle.

Laungani (2003) offers us a hypothetical case study which I include here as an example of the challenges he presents us with especially as it has a spiritual component to it.

This concerns an affluent Indian businessman, Mr Sharma and his wife Shakuntala, who live in Taipei, in Taiwan. The husband has testicular cancer, and he and his wife have come to London for his treatment. They have a daughter who is doing a Masters' degree at Princeton University, in New Jersey. The husband and wife lead relatively independent lives: he is totally absorbed with his business, and she, over the last 10 years has 'taken to' religion in a big way, to the neglect of all else. Much to her husband's unvoiced annoyance she has built a small temple in their large flat in Taipei, to which she invites all her Indian friends. Prayer meetings are held every day, devotional songs are sung, and visiting spiritual gurus are feted and feasted with unfailing regularity. She has acquired the reputation of being a holy person.

During her husband's post-operative convalescence in London, she visits all the temples, meets a variety of Gurus, and eventually forms a strong attachment to a religious group 'The Brahmakumaris' in London. An alarming change has come over her. Sex, meat, alcohol, and television have become taboo subjects; she has taken to wearing plain white cotton saris; she spends most of the day either with the Brahmakumaris or at home, absorbed in prayers for her husband's recovery.

Mr Sharma, anxious about his own health, his business interests that he has left behind, and about his wife's 'sanity' contacts his daughter in New Jersey, asking her to come to London. In less than two days, the daughter gets in touch with you for help.

The immediate challenge presented by this case study is that of seeing the family as a unit rather than treating them only as individuals and perhaps refusing to work with more than one member of the family, so therapists without a background in family, systemic or relationship work will be in difficulties. The wife's spiritual devotion needs to be understood in religious terms as well as understood as possibly a communication to her family, especially her husband. It would be easy for a Western therapist to respond that one is not competent to work with such culturally challenging material or with a family unit and give up on the issues posed.

It raises the question of whether such work should be restricted to specialist counsellors and psychotherapists (or culturally matched therapists although that opens up a whole other area of debate) or whether we expect a generic therapist to be suitably equipped. However, I would not be confident that our basic therapist training programmes equip therapists to work sensitively and competently in cross-cultural issues especially when issues of religion and spirituality are raised.

It is too easy for a white Western trained therapist raised in a post-Christian culture to see religiously inclined clients from ethnic minorities as quaint and certainly as other rather than as self. My own engagement with other religious and spiritual traditions has led me to explore issues relating to my own religious and spiritual heritage. I have been led to find where I belong within my own traditions. Many of my white contemporaries have found their place within Eastern religions mainly Buddhism. It does feel that if we are unexplored about these issues we are ill equipped to help our clients. This feels so basic to therapist training that I should not need to state it but the ignorance around these matters among many therapists is disturbing. For example, there is a lot of unprocessed anti-Christian sentiments that are voiced that in many cases clearly point to painful unresolved childhood experiences.

What I notice about the development of my own understanding of spirituality, culture and therapy is that it is face to face meetings and friendship with people from differing cultures that has underpinned any significant reading that I have done on the topic. When I first directly encountered racism awareness training in the early 1980s one of the initial key learnings for me was a regret, a sorrow that racism had until then prevented me from making much contact with people from other cultures. Thankfully that has now changed. However, I am still struck in some settings – often the most prestigious ones (!) how few non-white faces are present is a point strongly made in Moore's (2002) best selling *Stupid White Men* who quotes from a study by economists Vedder, Gallaway and Clingaman which shows that the average income of a black American is 61 per cent less per year than that of the average white income. This is the same percentage difference as it was in 1880!

My own research

My qualitative study into therapy and healing (West 1995a, 1997) uncovered how much complementary medicines and spiritual healing practices were being used by white therapists in Britain. I produced a four stage model for combining therapy and healing (see Table 4.2).

Ten of my twenty-seven respondents in the study could be located at least some of the time at Stage four, suggesting that they were working a way that transcends both roles of therapist and healer. What is less clear is how my respondents made sense of this

TABLE 4.2   Four stage model for combining therapy and healing

Stages	Position of Practitioners
One	Practitioner is initially either therapist or healer
Two	Practitioner becomes both therapist and healer and uses both separately with different groups of clients
Three	Practitioner begins to integrate both
Four	True integration occurs and transcends both roles

transcendence, although three issues are particularly relevant here – the use of language, around supervision, the taboo around spirituality (West 1995a).

The language issue was particularly notable and problematic, as one respondent put it, echoing Ankrah's (2000, 2002) more recent research, 'the problem with our present society and why we're having problems with people having spiritual emergencies is because we don't have a language or a concept here in mainstream society'. Another said that no label existed for the area of his work that encompassed the spiritual and that, 'we haven't got practitioners of what you are talking about'. I think we have but we do not have the language to easily discuss these matters in. This point was underlined by a third respondent who remarked, 'if you have absolutely no religion, I've noticed this in clients of a certain age . . . they actually don't have a lingo of their own for their own void, or spiritual wonder. And I see that as a handicap. At least I have a whole lot of words which might have some meaning . . . I do see a real suffering almost of people who don't have the vocabulary and they also don't know that I may have an inkling of what they are on about.' Again there are echoes here in Ankrah's story of needing the words, needing to know that spiritual emergencies were an extraordinary part of ordinary life in many cultures of the world. Swinton (2001) in discussing mental health care and spirituality comments on the practitioner's need to be fluent in the two languages involved – that of spirituality and that of psychiatry and psychology.

With regard to supervision eight out of the twenty-seven respondents reported various difficulties that had arisen in supervision of their work (further details in West 2000b). These varied, for example, there was one who did not take a particular client to supervision because 'it was quite difficult to deal with, being supervised by someone who had no sense of the spiritual'. I found this unethical

behaviour most disturbing and I was left wondering why the practitioner could not seek some sort of consultative supervision for
this one particular client. The practitioner had been proactive in
establishing a group of trainee therapists who met to discuss the
spiritual dimensions of their work.

Another had given up on the possibility of ever being truly
understood in terms of how they worked. This last respondent
commented, 'I do feel that I am constantly having to turn myself
inside out and upside down and back to front, to create it from
inside my guts. It feels my very being is the soil from which things
are created' (West 1995a p. 302). I do wonder what the long-term
implications are for people whose therapeutic work around spirituality is not being effectively supervised and supported. At the very least
their work with clients may be less effective, and I suspect the therapist's health and well-being might well be compromised. It is
interesting how Geller's (2001, Geller and Greenberg 2002)
research into presence mentioned above highlights self care by the
therapist as a factor in being able to offer presence. Notice in
Chapter 6 how Janet Muse-Burke talks about the difficulties in
finding a supervisor in the USA who was accepting of spirituality.

Nick Ladany, a leading US researcher into therapeutic supervision, recently stated at the Society for Psychotherapy Research
(International) Conference in Santa Barbara in June 2002 that
when supervisees are asked about their experience of supervision
the response is: one-third say it is excellent, one-third it was good
enough and one-third reply that it is problematic in some way. So
these supervision difficulties around therapy, healing and spirituality
can be considered in a broader perspective that acknowledges that
supervision is problematic (West 2003a).

Colin Feltham points to a number of problems with supervision
as it is understood within the counselling and psychotherapy world
in Britain. These are: 'thoughtlessly reinforcing practice traditions
and becoming an empty ritual; not being capable of dealing with
the challenges of our many different theoretical orientations; stifling
autonomy via mandatory mechanisms; having no known empirical
support for its effectiveness; not necessarily protecting clients; not
necessarily serving the needs of experienced practitioners; and too
easily becoming a social-psychological and sociological blindspot
for the profession' (2002 p. 26).

Feltham further suggests that supervision is 'at least partially a form
of surveillance and is associated with professional bureaucracy...

Supervision by its nature creates micro-cultures of conformity and mediocrity. Anecdotally there is ample evidence of supervisees feeling cowed, deskilled and wary in relation to supervision, however skilled and ethically competent the supervisor. This is because supervision is an institution in which we are at risk of infantilisation' (2002 p. 27).

I did a further study into therapy and spirituality in 1995–1996 into the spirituality of Quaker therapists (West 1998a) that showed that out of eighteen interviewed five had some issue or difficulty around supervision. If both studies are combined, supervision difficulties were present for 14 of them – nearly 30 per cent (West 2000b). In a situation where people volunteer to be interviewed it is likely that those with difficulties may well be more likely to offer themselves as research participants. Nevertheless a key theme of both the studies was around the taboo that exists around talking about spirituality. Perhaps like clients, supervisees are waiting to be given permission to talk of spirituality. Those facing the problems were as likely to be seasoned therapists as those not reporting such difficulties, both averaging over ten years in practice as therapists.

One therapist told me: 'There are moments I think when you almost feel a presence...I feel most humbled by those experiences, it's almost like, being present to something that's really beyond what you could do, there is a sense of at one-ness...This would not be easy to share with my supervisor.' This sense of a spiritual dimension or reality that is present in the therapeutic work but not welcome in supervision is reflected in the following comment by another respondent, an experienced therapist: 'The work I do there [in a voluntary agency] I'm circumspect in how I work with my supervisor...I'm cautious there. It's about wanting to remain credible...I think my supervisor would be right to question if I wanted to spend too much time on what are for me questions about my own practice, contextualising my work within the spiritual dimension.' Thankfully that has not been my recent experience in supervision where the contexualisation of spirituality has been a key feature of my own exploring and of my clients (West 2002b).

As mentioned in the last chapter Peter Gubi (2002) did a survey into the use of prayer by just over half of BACP accredited practitioners and 43 per cent (247) responded. In their work 59 per cent had used or used prayer covertly with clients (Christian or otherwise) and 12 per cent had used prayer overtly with Christian clients. Only 24 per cent who used prayer overtly or covertly had ever discussed

it in supervision. Gubi speculates that this may be '
is perceived to be a culturally unacceptable aspect
with the result that they fear 'their competence, p
and credibility is questioned, or in case it is badly 1
understood' (2000 p. 6). I am struck by how much prayer is actually
happening or has happened, and given the ongoing controversy
and debate about its use (Gubi 2001, 2002, 2003) it is clearly
unethical when therapists are using it with clients for it not be
explored in subsequent supervision. Also in the context of making
sense of the use of prayer in therapy a reluctance to talk about it
makes it rather hard to integrate its use into some therapeutic model.

The tension around prayer and supervision is discussed by Rose
(2002) who comments: 'There may be difficulties in supervision if
the counsellor is accepting of the client's need to pray, but the
supervisor feels that the counsellor is missing a valuable opportunity
to the client to explore the feelings that lie behind what is being
said' (pp. 48–49). Rose also recognises the potential for prayer to
complement supervision: 'Prayer is not a substitute for supervision, but some of those who pray experience it as providing similar
support in difficult situations' (p. 20).

Having presented these models and other ways of making sense
of the psychospiritual territory, I feel a bit like a mirror image of
how Moses must have felt when after 40 years in the wilderness he
finally led his people to the Promised Land but was not himself
able to enter. In my case I feel I do inhabit the psychospiritual
territory, at least some of the time, but my presenting of maps and
discussion of the territory does not of itself lead you (the reader),
into this land of promise. Only you can make that journey. My hope
here is not to have confused your journeying.

Therapy as a faith journey

Therapists work with their clients making a disciplined use of their
own selves. This is particularly so within the humanistic and
transpersonal approaches but it is also very true of the psychodynamic and psychoanalytic traditions. Val Wosket (1999) has
written about this therapeutic use of the self, posing the question: how
can counsellors and psychotherapists foster the growth of their own
unique helping potential? The metaphor of life as a journey whether
applied to therapist or client has much currency especially within
the person-centred tradition. This tradition and the existential one

talk about becoming a person (part of the title of a book by Carl Rogers (1961)). Therapist then can be seen as having a developing, evolving self.

I am only one among a number of writers (e.g. Tart and Deikman 1991) who have focused on the similarities between pursuing the spiritual life and the discipline of being a therapist. Consider how a working therapist will be devoting a lot of time and energy to being highly aware and focused on their clients' behaviour, posture, emotions, words – how and what is said and so on. Such a therapist will be also monitoring their reactions to their clients in all aspects of their being whether they conceptualise this as being counter transference, projective identification, congruence or whatever. All of this is meant to be done with at least a modicum of detachment or bracketing. This whole process is akin to a number of spiritual practices relating to self awareness including the Buddhist practice of mindfulness.

In a spiritual tradition like Buddhism such mindfulness practised assiduously over many years would inevitably produce a spiritual harvest. Even without a conscious and explicit focus on spirituality it is not surprising that a number of seasoned therapists do discuss spirituality in their life and work as they get older, for example (Jung 1967, Reich 1969, Rogers 1980, Chaplin 1989, Rowan 1993, Symington 1994, Heron 1998, Thorne, 2002). However, there is little discussion of spirituality in the common models of human development used like Erikson's (1977) or in models of therapist development like Stoltenberg and Delworth's (1988). The clearest most spiritual model is probably that provided by Ken Wilber – discussed above although interestingly he is not a practising therapist.

Another aspect of the work of the therapist that can impact on their souls is the day in day out wrestling with the pain, agonies, sufferings and traumas of their fellow humans. It is a massive challenge to do this work for many years without growing too thick a skin or without burning out. Montgomery's (1991) research into exemplar nurses is of interest here as she found that it was the spiritually active nurses who did not burn out – matching Geller's experienced practitioners who linked their own use of meditation to being able to offer presence to the clients. Vaughan (1991) warns us of the dangers of working out of our own wounds, to her the therapist should develop beyond being a wounded healer to becoming a whole and healed person.

My own experience as a full-time therapist (1979–1992) included feeling that not only was my own development fast tracked (which sometimes caused me to be out of step and kilter with those close to me) but also that sometimes the scars of my own wounds were freshly opened up by being with my clients and their sufferings. The cure was to not work full-time as a therapist and trainer and also to devote much more time and energy to my own self care.

There is a question of fit here between client and therapist. Fifty years of comparative research into the effectiveness of differing therapies suggests that there is not much to choose between any of the main schools of therapy across a wide range of client problems (discussed in Shapiro *et al.* 2000). Such randomised controlled trials continue and are expensive and eat up the limited research funds that I regard as unethical use of resources (West 2002a). The focus of research needs to shift more thoroughly to the individual therapist as advocated by Arbuckle back in 1968! This is something that the increasingly widespread use of outcome evaluation measures like the CORE questionnaire (Mellor-Clark *et al.* 2001) make possible. The challenge then is to find the best fit between client and therapist in the light of the individual therapist's development. Out of such thinking could emerge even more effective outcomes for the clients involved. This approach would be especially important for spiritually inclined clients.

This chapter has developed notions relating to understanding the psychospiritual territory and also the psychospiritual development of the individual therapist and its implications for her or his practice. In the next chapter we will consider the client's story in so far as it includes the spiritual.

Chapter 5

The Clients' Story

Hardly anyone has ever asked clients what they think about the counselling or psychotherapy they are receiving.

(McLeod 1990 p. 1)

As a client, I would prefer to work with a therapist who is 'present', and who believes in mystery and enchantment, rather than with one who thinks in terms of 'what is wrong with' me and believes that he has the ability to explain it to me.

(Sands 2000 p. 197)

In my first session I remember seeing myself as a black hole. Towards the end of my journey I saw myself as a gold line. I see it as a journey from a dark claustrophobic watery hole, to the top of the water, and I splash out as a golden fish.

(West 1994a p. 300)

In this chapter I explore the clients' story and how we can support our clients' spirituality in whatever form that might take and what difficulties might arise. I draw on my own experiences with clients, research and other relevant literature. The focus is always on the client's understanding, experience and use of spirituality and to what extent the counselling process feels spiritual to her or him.

Change or gnosis: what does the client want?

Things had become too much. The sadness and self-doubt I felt could not be contained any more and I was scared and knew that I needed to talk to someone who could help me sort out all the feelings and confused emotions I felt.

A sense that somewhere inside me was a me striving to get out
and to get in touch. A knowledge that my life wasn't right or
full.

> (Two respondents answering why they
> sought therapy, West 1994a p. 297)

With the apparent convergence of therapy approaches towards an
acceptance of the crucial importance of the therapeutic relationship
or alliance as a key outcome variable coupled with various surveys
showing increasing numbers of therapists committed to an integrative or eclectic way of working (Hollanders 1997), it might be
easy to think that all roads lead to Rome, with the implication that
all clients are on the same journey. Indeed it is the differing views
of what constitutes the good life that still separate the major
schools of counselling and psychotherapy. Freud's oft quoted, if
slightly tongue in cheek dictum that the purpose of psychoanalysis
is to turn neurotic unhappiness into everyday misery is so far away
from the self-actualisation advocated by Rogers, not to mention
the developing of the Higher Self of the transpersonal approaches.
All of this can seem so far away from a client who wishes practical
help with their panic attacks.

One way of bringing all of this into one overarching theory
was achieved by Ken Wilber whose model I explored in the last
chapter. The key feature of Wilber's 10 stage model of human
development, is that there are problems associated with each stage
of human development, and that a particular form and style of
therapeutic approach is needed and indeed most useful for each
stage.

Wilber rather arrogantly (if probably accurately!) insists that
secular Western therapy can only help a client on the early stages
of his model and that more specifically spiritual ways of working
with human development are needed to get further. Wilber also
acknowledges that overly spiritual forms of helping may not be as
useful as secular therapy for the basic issues of human living.

This then gives a way of viewing our clients' therapeutic needs
which can range from very basic questions like: how do I walk
down the street without having a panic attack, through questions
like: how can I cope with the feelings aroused in me since the death
of my partner, to more explicitly existential or spiritual questions
such as: my life has lost all meaning, or did God want me to have
a miscarriage?

For many of us (clients) various questions from different stages of our development can be tangled up together when we seek therapy. Indeed my own experience is that we do not always consciously know the deepest reasons we are seeking therapy at the first encounter with our therapists. Some times a client will stop after sorting out one set of problems recognising that there is further therapeutic work but will say: 'I am not ready at this stage to open that can of worms just yet'.

So the situation can change over time – we might begin with a need for better adjustment to an existing but difficult situation; we might then seek change rather than adjustment with all that that involves; and at a later stage gnosis might be all that satisfies us. Our therapeutic journey might well not be as clear and as linear as this. Indeed some will be happy with just one stage for years if not a life time.

What do I mean by gnosis? To me it is akin to mystical illumination, a deep knowing of the truth of life, including my own, an unflinching look at the true nature and mystery of things which I take to be deeply spiritual for want of another, perhaps better, word.

Some examples from my practice

I first of all want to present a lengthy case study based upon my work with a client whom I call Matthew (a fuller contextualised version can be found in West 2003b) who has kindly agreed with me to write about him here and who has approved the details and discussion that follows. I should state clearly that this is my view of part of what transpired during Matthew's therapy with me and Matthew has a very different story to tell which precedes my commentary on his therapy with me.

The client, Matthew (named and some personal details changed) was in his early 30s of mixed race origins but was raised within a white working-class family. Although brought up within a fairly devout Christian (Church of England) family, Matthew had become a Sufi in his adult life, and had regular contact with his Sufi teacher or master. His spiritual life was of great importance to him, and he would quote from Sufi poets like Rumi during his therapy sessions. However, it was many months into his therapy with me that he chose to reveal his religious orientation (see below). He was working as a psychiatric nurse at the time of his therapy with me.

Matthew's immediate presenting issue was that of tension with a female manager that was affecting his performance at work. He also reported that he was 'out of touch with his feelings', and had some sense of 'not taking his place in the world'. He said that he did not feel grown up, and was not 'coming into his power'. He also expressed regret that he was not married or in a committed long-term sexual relationship.

Matthew spent his first 6 weeks of life being looked after by Christian nuns in an orphanage. He was then adopted. Matthew described himself as a bit rebellious as an adolescent and early adult and as an under-achiever at school. In his early 20s he had worked as a freelance journalist on a local paper developing a reputation for articles that had an angry and political edge to them. He resumed his studies in his mid-20s, and chose nursing, and realised that he had found his vocation.

However, it soon seemed very clear to me that although he was making an apparent success of his working life, he felt that was not realising his full potential both at work and in his life as a whole. He felt particularly keenly the fact that he was not married nor in a committed relationship, yet had a deep connection to his adopted Christian family where being married and having a family was expected. Matthew was living in Manchester on his own, but made regular visits at the weekend to his parents some miles away where a Sunday family meal usually occurred. Whilst such family life fits the Christian sub-culture he was brought up in, and felt he belonged to, it also emphasised how young he still seemed. Questions often arose around whether or when he was going to meet a nice Christian girl and settle down.

With Matthew there seemed a basic developmental issue of why he was not progressing into adulthood and starting a family that seemed to form the basis of his therapy with me. This involved an exploration of his thoughts and feelings about his experience and understanding of his adoption, his early childhood, and also his difficult and sometimes rebellious adolescence. I felt at times like a mentor, older brother or parent. At other times I felt more like a fellow traveller on the spiritual and therapeutic journey.

Matthews sometimes seemed to take up my suggestions too readily, something which I explored in supervision: was I becoming too much of an expert for him? It seemed clear that in fact he was taking up that which was of use to him, making it his own, developing it further for himself in his own unique way.

Rather than cover Matthew's therapy with me in some detail, which to do it justice would take a whole book, I have decided to select some parts of the case narrative that especially reflect the spiritual interventions used. However, it must be recognised that much of the work could be seen and understood in fairly conventional therapeutic terms, but also that for Matthew and myself this was a therapeutic encounter that was infused with spirituality and reflected the spiritual paths and spiritual journey we both saw ourselves as being on. From this perspective the whole of life is both sacred and spiritual.

I have, after consultation with Matthew, chosen not to focus on most aspects of both his family and his work life within this case study. It seemed especially and ethically important to gain Matthew's explicit permission to draw on his case material in a way that felt appropriate to him, for even by changing some of the details the client could still feel uncomfortable with publication of their experiences. (I have explored issues relating to ethics in therapy and therapy research elsewhere (West 2002a).)

However, it does need to be acknowledged how important the therapeutic work was around his adoption. Previous therapeutic work with adopted clients had alerted me to how less firmly rooted or grounded they might feel. It felt as if the work around his adoption was a necessary prelude to him being able to move on developmentally in his life. It also raised profound spiritual questions some of which were explored in the session alluded to above.

Inevitably the early sessions were spent in hearing something of his story, why he had come for counselling and an exploration of some immediate issues at work. To give a flavour of these early sessions I shall include some extracts from my case notes at the time:

First session   At work in the multi-disciplinary team it had been easier for him this last week but he felt that his spiritual side was still not fully acceptable, however he had challenged a woman who he felt was trying to shame him. He read me a poem he had written which I was very moved by. Apparently I am the only person he can talk to about his spirituality outside of the weekly meditation group he belongs to. His work with me is getting more explicitly spiritual.

Next session   He said that he feels he is now more authentic, more his true self, and he offered a powerful image of him spiritually climbing a ladder to heaven, but having other bits to his self that were maybe left behind.

I feel that he is still telling me so little, but he is talking about things he tells no one else, and I value his sharing them with me and I hope that I convey this to him. I praised him for the poem from our last session and said how it stayed with me all week but it was very hard for him to accept this praise. He told me a moving Sufi story that I compared to the death of Jesus.

One week later He said he was not ready to face the truth about his adoption and what it meant to him. Clearly, despite his feeling of not being ready, he is beginning the therapeutic and spiritual journey but it feels painful and difficult.

Next session Perhaps this is a real turning point, he was angry with God in the session, and I feel that this could just help to begin to heal issues about his adoption.

There were also several key moments some months into his therapy. In one session I was moved to share with him that his spirituality had a feeling or flavour of the Middle East or Istanbul, a sense of a place where East meets West. This reflected my feeling, which I had not expressed to him, that his spirituality was in some way different to Christianity. (In retrospect it also could have reflected his mixed race origins.) He was pleased by what I said, and shared the fact that he was a Sufi. Looking back on his therapy there was a pattern of him choosing when to share key aspects of himself with me. A similar withholding occurred later in relation to him telling me about a key sexual relationship from his past.

It is interesting to reflect that one way of understanding Quakers is to see them as essentially a mystical group (Jones 1921) indeed the Quaker focus on experiencing God, on the value of silently waiting (Gillman 1988) underlines this viewpoint. Likewise, Sufis are considered also as representing the mystical tradition within Islam. This I think made it more possible for Matthew and I to share the frequent silences that appeared to have a huge therapeutic value for him during his sessions with me. I think this shared mystical focus on experiencing the Divine and on awaiting for Divine guidance gave us a common spiritual or theological base with which to work with. I was consequently less challenged spiritually by Matthew than some of my other spiritually minded clients of a different religious outlook to my own. It was as if with Matthew we simply shared the spiritual nature of our encounter rather than trying to make a shared theological sense of it, a focus on experiencing rather than on theorising or theologising.

One session soon after this he said that he was afraid of the 'spiritual intimacy' that was occurring between us. I was much struck by this phrase. Exploring what this meant, he referred to the silences that arose in our sessions that had a healing effect on him, the synchronous way words and images that overlapped came to both of us, and the feelings of interconnectedness that especially arose in the silences. It seemed important to me to check out with him what role he was experiencing me in as I was wary of in anyway becoming his spiritual director and what that could mean. He replied that I was his counsellor, that he had a spiritual teacher but that because his spirituality was important to him he wanted to be able to explore it in his therapy with me. I was relieved to hear this.

A few sessions later I had an experience in the silence with him of dropping into a very deep place that I can, and do, reach on occasions in meditation or spiritual contemplation. I felt that I was on the edge of going so deep that I would lose all ordinary consciousness. I knew that it was not appropriate for me to go any deeper in the middle of a counselling session but I was reluctant to bring myself out of being on the edge of this very deep and very spiritual space. I was thus able to relate to him from that deep space. It seemed very important. I assumed that my going there had a meaning, it was not just an accident. It felt important to stay there in that deep space and not to break contact or consciousness. I did find a way of speaking to him from that deep space without losing it. I felt that I was on an edge, I could go either deeper into the space or come back to a more ordinary way of relating. It was almost as if I was on the edge of falling or dropping down inside myself which felt almost physically located. In that moment I did not quite know what this meant. It was, I think, part of that spiritual intimacy that he had referred to earlier, and part of that was not always knowing exactly what was going on, but trusting in the spiritual process that was unfolding. Some of it, I think, was saying to him that this is OK, that it was OK for him to be in a similar deep and spiritual space. At some level it felt like a kind of mentoring, being in silence with him from a deep space, not having to come out of it, staying with that space and with him at the same time. There was something different about being there with him in that session and an extraordinary feeling of 'holding' that deep space, not having to come out of it, and not going so deep that I lost that connection. It felt risky but very important.

Although he had explored his difficulties at work all through his therapy with me, especially working within a large multi-disciplinary, multicultural team the full story did not emerge for many months. He had been blamed and had subsequently felt both ashamed and angry for a mistake that had occurred at work. The mistake was for something that was not truly his fault. It seemed especially important that this whole area of his experience could be safely brought out into the light of day within his therapy with me. Clearly the whole incident had proven damaging to him and his relationships with colleagues. The challenge to him was to find a place within, from which he could forgive and self-forgive. This all seemed part of a maturing process that also included him successfully applying for promotion to deputy in the nursing department he worked in.

Comments by Matthew

The question which cannot be answered

I went initially into the relationship not to seek God, nor to explore my spirituality; I came for one thing and in the long run, I got something else. I did not go to seek realisation of God through psychotherapy – but I was not willing also to deny the presence of the transcendent should it have occurred.

Like all relationships, what happens is often not what is expected – so from my own point of view the only construction I would go into the sessions with, was a few moments in my car before the meeting, of slowing down from the scatter of the busy working day and focusing on self. In hindsight, I feel it was simple choices like this which laid the ground for the opening of awareness.

I initiated the therapy because I had a question. I think I went along originally to marvel at the question, because the question felt like a warmth in my belly; like a pleasant meaningfulness. But the therapy could never answer the question – and that was as much a disappointment as anything. In truth the realisation that 'the question' could not be 'answered' was in itself a painful conclusion to the relationship for myself for a while; a source of frustration to my intellect.

To Be Is To Know

But I remember writing a short poem sometime round about the latter stages of the therapy entitled 'To Be Is To Know' – which even now impresses upon me the feeling that my existence cannot be rationalised. So the question which initially impelled me is itself eventually a source of knowing since it does not attempt to quantify but merely wishes to unfold, to become itself, to experience itself.

To Be Is To Know

I'm a liar. Merely
Trying to sound like
A man I attempt to be.

Setting it out in perfect straight lines,
Each sentence spoke on schedule;
Interpretations smooth as clockwork here
All my trains run on time.

But someone is caged
This other I am,
Whose excluded, imprisoned, exiled:

Someone is caged
This other I am,
Whose excluded, imprisoned.

Exiled:
This enemy in my empire,
This plague in my palace of mannequins.
This firestorm in my idol-temple of 'I'-
His freedom would be catastrophe,
Since what he conveys in a sigh
Unpicks my grim industry,

He would turn me away from the lights of my town
Toward that dark district,
Past the old mines and library

And then to that realm of the rough
Silent river, where

Hooded truth,
Patient in twilight sits
Waiting for me
With his minstrel
Beneath
Leafy trees,
On moonlit ground.

Spiritual intimacy

Like sunlight on the ocean; it is both whilst appearing in different forms. Neither one nor the other, counsellor and client, two human beings meeting with no other purpose than their ontological recognition of both self and other. In that sense, we are both the sunlight and the ocean.

Remembering beauty

Because there are moments in my life when we disappear. This is what I could only describe as 'spiritual intimacy' – a time of tangible presence, of gentleness and stillness; sunlight on the ocean. The therapy in these times became a praising of moments of wonder in my childhood: my grandmother's house, an empty playground on a bright spring afternoon, or a walk through falling snow with the family dog. In truth, a recognition of these life experiences is as therapeutic for me as much, if not more than, cause-and-effect analysis.

The spiritual intimacy between us allowed these memories and the attendant emotions to surface without analysis or interpretation. It was a recognition of myself as a truth – a truth which transcends for a moment, question and answer, and is instead, a sublime acceptance, and an inward sense of perfection. Naturally that is a sense which is impossible to convey to another except through silence and stillness.

Commentary on Matthew's therapy

Matthew's comments above have a poetic quality about them that does some kind of justice both to who he is and to the nature of the therapy work he did with me. Some of Matthew's therapy could be seen in non-spiritual terms about a developmental need on his part, to heal the trauma of his adoption soon after birth, to deal with his difficulties at work, his need to find a sexual partner and so on. However, this misses the truth that Matthew saw himself as being on a spiritual path, that he chose to have therapy with me because of my spiritual approach to therapy and that there was for both of us some explicitly spiritual experiences and spiritual content in the therapeutic encounter.

It could prove helpful to consider the spiritual aspects of my therapeutic work with Matthew in the light of the list of possible spiritual intervention in therapy put forward by Richards and Bergin. Their list is as follows:

Praying for clients, encouraging clients to pray, discussing theological concepts, making references to scriptures, using spiritual relaxation and imagery techniques, encouraging forgiveness, helping clients live congruently with their spiritual values, self-disclosing spiritual beliefs or experiences, consulting with religious leaders, and using religious bibliotherapy.

(Richards and Bergin 1997 p. 128)

Considering these items in turn:

1   *Praying for clients.*   I did not specifically pray for Matthew, as I never felt that he was especially in need of prayer during or after his therapy sessions with me. I did on several occasions pray during a session that I would be of best use for him at moments when things seemed especially stuck or difficult.

2   *Encouraging clients to pray.*   This did not seem appropriate at all. Matthew had his own active spiritual life that I knew included meditation and other spiritual practices that I was not fully party to. I also only have somewhat limited knowledge of Islam and of Sufism.

3   *Discussing theological concepts.*   This did occur on occasions, very often at Matthew's prompting.

4   *Making references to scriptures.*   Again fairly often at Matthew's prompting and occasionally at mine.

5   *Using spiritual relaxation and imagery techniques.*   Not as such but in the occasions described above spiritual relaxation could be said to be implicitly happening.

6   *Encouraging forgiveness.*   Yes in both the sense that Matthew needed to forgive members of his work team for their unwarranted attack on him over the alleged 'mistake' discussed above, and his subsequent anger towards them, and, in a more defuse sense, the way I encouraged Matthew to self-forgive for not achieving, not becoming the full-fledged person that he was capable of being. I discuss the whole issue of forgiveness in therapy more fully in Chapter 8.

7   *Helping clients live congruently with their spiritual values.* This was implicitly and sometimes explicitly a key feature of Matthew's therapeutic work with me.

8   *Self-disclosing spiritual beliefs or experiences.*   This was an important aspect of trust building especially in the early stages of our work together.

9   *Consulting with religious leaders.*   This did not seem appro-
     priate or necessary.
10 *Using religious bibliotherapy.*   This did not arise.

In my discussion in the last chapter of these spiritual interventions
of Richards and Bergin (West 2000a) I added two extra ones –
asking religious and spiritual questions during assessment and the
rather broadly based 'use of spiritual intuition or inspiration'
which, I feel, was a key feature of Matthew's therapy with me. There
is a growing body of literature and research that covers spiritual
moments in psychotherapy (e.g. Rogers 1980, Mearns and Thorne
1988, Thorne 1991, 2002, Rowan 1993, Richards and Bergin 1997,
West 1997, 1998a, 2000a). Rogers (1980), in particular, spoke of
his experience of what he called 'presence' which was explored in
the last chapter that I will briefly summarise here: 'I find that when
I am closer to my inner, intuitive self...whatever I do seems to be
full of healing. Then simply my presence is releasing and helpful...
At these moments it seems that my inner spirit has reached out
and touched the spirit of the other...Profound growth and healing
energies are present.'

Was this experience described by Rogers a version of the 'spiritual
intimacy' that Matthew feared? Does it not also encompass the
deep spiritual and meditative space that I found myself in with
Matthew in the session described above? I think both are true. Brian
Thorne (1991) speaks of special spiritual moments in therapy akin
to Rogers' presence that he calls 'tenderness'. Significantly Thorne
states that he no longer had to 'leave my eternal soul outside the
door' of the counselling room, and that he could now 'capitalize
on many hours spent in prayer and worship' (Mearns and Thorne
1988 p. 37). It seems to me that my openness about wanting to work
explicitly around spirituality with my clients had a similar healing
effect on my own splitting off of some aspects of my spiritual nature
from my therapist self such as Thorne has described.

To perhaps extend this further we could see whether these
spiritual moments in Matthew's therapy with me were akin to
Buber's I/Thou relationship discussed in the previous chapter. We
need to be mindful of Buber's assertion that the therapeutic encounter
cannot be truly I/Thou, given the power imbalance in the relationship between client and therapist, nevertheless it does seem to me
to have something of the flavour of an I/Thou moment. Richard, a
Gestalt psychotherapist, whom I interviewed during my researches

into therapy and healing spoke at length about the I/Thou relationship as it occurred in his therapy work: 'It is ever changing,
I mean each moment is unique and each pair of people is unique.
So it is difficult to put it into structured words other than to say
that one of the factors is a sense of absorption with the client, with
the process, like how children become very absorbed with things
and oblivious to the background...I would feel very alert or very
aware...very attuned with the client, very empathic with their
feelings, very quick to sense what they are feeling. Sometimes even
quicker than them.'

I later asked him if in this I/Thou he and the client were still
separate or merged. He replied 'both' and went on to say: 'in the
I/Thou we are one, yet there is also a sense in which we are still
separate. I think it may be a problem where we are trying to use
language to define things that aren't easily defined. For me anyway
there's a sense of joinedness, of absorption with the client but also
a sense of still being grounded and separate'. This I think chimes
in well with my description above of going into a deep place inside
myself but still staying connected to Matthew.

I learnt a lot about working with my clients' spirituality through
working with Matthew. I also learnt a lot about my own spirituality.
It was a challenging and rewarding experience to share his spiritual
unfolding. It was, and is, a rare privilege to share that aspect of my
nature so frequently in the human encounter that is the therapeutic
relationship.

From Matthew's case study, the reader might draw the false conclusion that working with the client's spirituality inevitably involves
long-term therapeutic work. In my experience openness to the
client's spirituality broadly does not change the number of sessions
of therapy the client has. In some cases the inclusion of the client's
spirituality seemed to shorten the number of sessions they needed.

Being open to our clients' spirituality can be part of a one-off
session, part of brief solution-focused therapy or an integral part of
long-term psychoanalysis. From my viewpoint therapy is a process
of unfolding of issues by the client in the presence of the therapist.
It takes the time it takes, no more, no less. However, if the context
is an externally imposed rigid restriction to a small number of
sessions or a focus on a manualised treatment approach, the client's
spirituality might be excluded. A spiritually minded therapist working
in that context would then come face to face with the ethical issues
this would raise.

However, the research evidence to 'prove' that manualised treatment works better than non-manualised therapy does not exist. (We have known for a number of years about the equivalence of outcome, namely that when differing therapies are compared working with the same client problems, there is little to choose (discussed in Shapiro *et al.* 2000).) Nor do we know that fixed short-term limits on therapy are cost effective.

I would like to be able to prove that working with the client's spirituality provides better and quicker outcomes. I cannot as yet prove this gut feeling to be true and somehow I doubt if it will ever be established. However, I strongly suspect that spiritually minded clients prefer their spirituality to be included in their therapy. As Richards and Bergin (1997) insist: If it is important to them why not use it to help them?

Further examples

A second example from my practice is of a woman who had had several counselling sessions with me in the mid-1980s. Early in 1991 she rang me up out of the blue to say that she was staying on a remote Scottish island and having some kind of spiritual emergency (Grof and Grof 1989) that involved her throwing herself off the harbour wall into the sea on a daily basis as some kind of cleansing ritual. I found out that she was staying in a house that belonged to the Findhorn Community and was receiving plenty of skilled support. So there was no need for me to leap into my car and dash up to Scotland. However, in those counselling sessions with me she had first become aware of herself as having a spiritual side and so she regarded me as her spiritual godfather. In her current phase of spiritual emergency it was important and grounding for her to make contact with me.

With a recent client, the challenge has been to support her as she faced a deep seated need to leave the job she was in and to trust that a new life would then emerge. Part of the challenge for me was to face the echoes from my own major life changes of a decade ago, to use my own experiences to help understand her but to not use them to push her process of change in any particular direction. I also had to face the uncomfortable feeling that I was experiencing such a push myself once again and to not deny this to myself since by so doing I might become less open to her changes. I have had to wait and allow her to be the author of her own life and not taking any power or responsibility from her but to reflect back to her what I heard her telling me verbally and non-verbally. I was ever mindful of these issues and took them regularly to supervision. The spiritual issue of being her true self and embracing her spiritual journey and destiny and facing the lack of self-esteem and self-doubts involved was key to her making progress. It was so important to me that I could articulate her experiences within a spiritual but non-religious frame which matched her own worldview. It felt at times as if I was reminding her of this truth of hers namely that her changes were at root those of a spiritual nature involving her soul. By connecting with the spiritual truth of what was happening to her she could more easily deal with the self-doubts and residual lack of self-esteem that was holding her back.

With a number of other clients as well as these three mentioned above I feel that I was acting as a *spiritual witness* to the spiritual process that is happening to them. This is bit like being a midwife if you like only intervening when the process gets stuck but content to wait, listen and support a natural, healthy spiritual unfolding.

The challenge to the therapist: knowing yourself in relation to spirituality

I believe that being present to one's clients' spirituality necessitates that one knows oneself in relation to spirituality. This means being aware of what spirituality means to you both in positive, negative and indifferent ways. For example, it has been shown from research in the USA (Propst *et al.* 1992) that atheist or agnostic therapists are as capable as religiously minded therapists of successfully using religious imagery with devout clients. In contrast Allman *et al.* found in their survey of 285 US therapists' views of clients having mystical experiences that 'psychodynamic and behavioural thera-pists attributed significantly more pathology to such clients than did humanistic/existential therapists' (1992 p. 568). Furthermore they found that some of their respondents considered a client reporting mystical experiences 'possibly psychotic' regardless of the information presented.

The implication is that therapists need to have carefully exam-ined themselves around spirituality and around phenomena that their clients might well label as 'spiritual' including experiences outside and within the counselling session. Closely related to this is being aware of one's counter-transference material that arises in response to one's clients' spirituality as recommended by Lannert (1991) who found that few therapists in the USA had had any training around spiritual and religious issues and relied instead on their own convictions to guide their work in these areas with clients.

As an example of my own bias, I usually have an immediate positive reaction to someone who shares the same faith group as I do. This changes as I learn which wing of my faith they occupy! Likewise I tend to have a negative reaction to people who treat sacred texts as the word of God without any discussion. However, as therapists we need to see the person behind this façade, tune into their truth, gain an understanding of why they hold the position they hold and so on.

Knowing how it might be for the client

The challenge is to be present to the clients' spirituality, to be present to whatever that means for that client however bizarre and however fundamentalist their position is. This demands for me a phenomenological stance of respecting the client's truth, respecting their story, deeply listening to what they have to say including that which is not voiced out loud. This involves attempting the impossible task of bracketing, of putting aside my own assumptions, my own reactions to the words chosen by my client, to freely enter into their experience, their understandings.

I also, unlike some colleagues, believe there is value in my learning about different cultures and sub-cultures including a working knowledge of the main religions present in Britain and also of the New Religious Movements and New Age Spirituality. There is no substitute for hearing from my client how it is for them but I feel I owe it to them to have some working knowledge of what it means to be Islamic, Hindu, Sikh, Jewish and Christian in Britain today (e.g. Barker 1989, Davie 1994, Lartey 1997, Walker 1998, Laungani 2003).

Spiritual dilemmas can arise for clients which can prove to be very painful and challenging to their sense of self and spirituality. For people committed to a spiritual path, there are plenty of tensions and challenges in our postmodern society around living their faith. Apart from the more obvious dilemmas to Christians around sexual morality and arm sales I have noticed with a number of Buddhists that there can be a real tension between pursuing the spiritual life and being in a committed relationship or in one case following the spiritual path and having an active promiscuous sex life.

I think it is really important that we therapists take a tender approach to these sorts of dilemmas that can be most painful and challenging and not have any easy solutions. It is so important that we respect the spiritual faith involved. A close friend of mine who is Jewish and very committed to that way of life could not accept having his son circumcised and neither could his wife. So they devised a spiritual ceremony that welcomed their son without circumcision. Her parents refused to attend and it was a most painful time for all. There are no easy answers in such situations.

Dealing with arranged marriages can also be equally painful and admit no obvious solutions. Again it is crucial to respect the traditions involved and to view the dilemmas within the client's frame in which the tension the client experiences between following the cultural traditions of the family or that of the dominant white culture is hard to resolve without some sense of loss. This echoes the comments of Pittu Laungani in the last chapter in which he is seen as English in India and Indian in England.

In our work with our clients and their spirituality it is important that we maintain boundaries appropriate to therapy, that in a very deep sense we remain a therapist to our client and recognise those occasions when we may be close to either losing the boundary or over stepping it and have the necessary support to remain effective as therapist for the client involved or make effective use of supervision.

Supervision: is your supervisor open to your clients' spirituality and how you might work with it?

This should be self-evident and obvious, however my own researches (West 1997, 1998a, 2000b) referred to in Chapter 3 show how frequent it is that there is some dilemma, some issue that prevents therapists from getting effective supervision around working with their clients' spirituality. I strongly suspect that is part of a bigger issue picked up by other researchers (Ladany et al. 1999, Gubi 2000, Kaberry 2000, Tune 2001) of how therapists avoid taking issues to supervision of a kind which their supervisors will not be accepting, not be approving of.

Rowan (2001), as mentioned earlier, has written a paper that provides us with a framework and guidance for effective transpersonal supervision that is valuable to anyone with a spiritually informed approach to therapy whether transpersonal in orientation or not. It certainly represents one solution to the dilemmas raised by spiritually minded therapists with secular supervisors and gives some valuable information based on Grof's notion of spiritual emergency.

To save future trouble I would recommend that in the contracting process at the start of a new supervision relationship that therapists discuss their openness to their clients' spirituality and to exploring the same within the therapeutic relationship. This needs to involve checking out their supervisor's attitude to spirituality and its experience and exploration within therapy. It is also helpful if both supervisor and supervisee share a clear understanding of the boundaries of the therapy relationship with regard to spirituality – what is appropriate, when referral is necessary and so on. Exploring experiences of the I/Thou relationship (Buber 1970), Rogers' presence (Rogers 1980), Thorne's (1991) tenderness and the possible use of prayer (Gubi 2000) would all prove a helpful point of departure!

Referrals

All therapists need to know their limits including whom they can work with and what they are competent to work with any one client. Such knowledge should also include what the limits are to the therapy relationship including role limits, that is, at what point might they cease to be a therapist as such and become a spiritual teacher or director. Knowing who to refer to in such circumstances is crucial. As with any kind of client with any kind of problem, the therapist needs to know when they are out of their depth and once again appropriate supervision and appropriate contracting should help.

It is important to know when a client might benefit from faith-based help and it is valuable if the existence of such support has been located in the contracting process, or failing that the therapist or client can easily access the information. Many clients deliberately choose therapists who are not of their faith, sometimes, so they can explore faith issues without feeling judged, but there may be a time in their therapeutic process when faith-based help is appropriate.

Those of us used to working as part of a health-care team may find it not so challenging to include spiritual teachers and so on as part of the treatment package for a particular client. People's spiritual faith represent potentially a great resource for their health and well-being and it is foolish not to make best use of it to benefit the client.

Knowing where we stand: locating our work in relation to spirituality and therapy

The focus of this book is about how we can effectively and healthily honour our clients' spirituality within the therapeutic encounter. This demands I believe that we inform ourselves of the nature of human spirituality and such informing needs to occur on a holistic level and includes our own sense of being a spiritual self if at all possible.

One way of exploring where the boundary lies for therapists in relation to working with their clients' (and their own) spirituality is by considering the following extract from an email I received from a North American therapist. I should stress that it is only a brief extract from a longer email and that I have not as yet sought any clarifications about the statements made by this female therapist. As further background, the therapist is a Quaker and knows that I am also a Quaker and so this informs the way she responds to my question, asking her to illustrate her spiritual approach to therapy via a case example. I have shared this extract with a number of different therapists, supervisors and researchers over the years and received a range of responses (ranging from 'So what?' to 'Oh my God!') that have usually resulted in most fruitful discussions. The readers might wish to record their immediate reactions to this following text before reading any further.

Jane was noting where she was a year ago, and where she is now... She was feeling positive about what she saw, and said she felt blessed to have me in her life. (So much of this can't really be put into words because it was what was happening in the room that was beyond words.) I said, as I have felt strongly towards her, that I wanted to tell her that I loved her. She said she felt the same way about me. I said that I felt God had brought us into each other's lives. She told about going, as she does every week, to spend time sitting in a chapel, and having thanked God for bringing me into her life. Now, I know that in the professional world this is not how therapists are supposed to relateto clients... But I am trying to convey a moment in which we both experienced, acknowledged and expressed God's presence in our work together.

Now I want to approach exploring this text in a respectful manner and in a way that illuminates the focus of this book on therapy and spirituality. The therapist, let us call her Frances, is talking about a session in which her client Jane reviewed their work together. Jane had struggled with some difficult issues and was clearly acknowledging how much progress she had made with the help of her therapist Frances. Clearly they share a spiritual perspective on their lives and therapeutic work together although we do not know if they share the same religious faith since certainly in Britain Quakers attend meeting houses not chapels and Jane refers to a chapel in the text above.

Spiritually minded clients in effective therapy might well regard themselves as blessed in their therapist. Frances then tells us that much of what was happening in the therapy room was beyond words which is a familiar experience in relation to spirituality and therapy discussed elsewhere in this book. We should also keep this thought in mind that Frances is trying to verbalise something beyond words and if we focus too literally on the words we may be in error.

Frances then relates that she told Jane that she loved her. Is this a response to Jane's statement about feeling blessed to have Frances in her life? Might it also be partially a response to the (spiritual) atmosphere in the room, the being 'beyond words'. It is not clear. Some readers would find this statement by Frances as inappropriate, pointing to possible counter transference or in person-centred terms not staying with the client's process. We cannot be sure and we do not have Jane's version of events either. We do know that Jane said she felt the same way about Frances and we hope that this is an authentic response by her.

Frances then says that she felt God had brought us into each other's lives. This could be seen as an acknowledgement by Frances of what she had gained from being Jane's therapist and potentially a way of making the relationship more equal. Indeed it does not feel inappropriate within a spiritual therapeutic frame-work in which the client Jane has already said she felt blessed to have Frances in her life. The God language will be a turn-off to secular therapists but in a therapeutic encounter between these two people who both clearly value the spiritual, such a use of language is congruent.

Jane then tells Frances how she goes every week to spend time in a chapel and having thanked God for bringing Frances into her life. I get uneasy at this point as I always do when any client or student thinks I am too wonderful. It feels such a statement needs to be considered in the context of transference and its implications for the therapeutic relationship and whether if unprocessed it will impede Jane's progress.

Frances now acknowledges to me in the email text that this is not how therapists are supposed to relate to clients. Her awareness of this matter might then indicate that she would take the matter to supervision (unlikely, as US therapists do not usually have supervision after registration) but perhaps she would discuss it with colleagues or reflect further on her own. She then concludes by affirming what she was trying to convey to me, namely a sense of God's presence in her work with Jane that they both acknowledged.

That brings us to the crux of this issue: Is this possibly a healthy experience of spirituality? Is any encounter of a spiritual nature healthy and appropriate to psychotherapy? How one answers these questions is crucial and it is vitally important to the clients involved.

Conclusion

Being present to one's clients' spirituality in whatever form it takes for them can represent a real challenge to one's own worldview. Indeed, it can act as a spur to one's own journeying into the realms of the spirit. Such work with a client necessitates careful supervision from someone suitably experienced. To many of us the spiritual represents perhaps the most important part of our lives and beings and is thereby clearly a most appropriate matter for the therapeutic encounter.

Chapter 6
Relevant Issues

To further explore the meaning of being alive to our clients' spirituality I will in this chapter focus on a number of relevant issues including: a consideration of spiritual interventions in therapy with a particular focus on forgiveness; the spiritual issues arising from bereavement; and the use of retreats. Finally I considered the context in which people seek therapeutic help relating to their spirituality.

Spiritual interventions in therapy

> Although significant efforts have been made to develop and implement religious and spiritual interventions into psychotherapy practice, the profession is still in its infancy in this domain.
>
> (Richards and Bergin 1997 p. 256)

Despite the reluctance in some quarters to acknowledge healthy spirituality there is a growing interest in the spiritual dimension of counselling and in the integration of spiritual interventions into mainstream counselling (West 2000a). Richards and Bergin (1997) suggest that because of the continued interest in spirituality among the general population, there is a need for therapists to challenge the historical alienation between religion and psychotherapy. I have argued in this book for therapists to be open to their clients' spirituality. Whilst such receptivity is often apparent within pastoral counselling (Lynch 2000), the current alienation of many people in Britain from traditional religion (Davie 1994) means that for many people the counsellor has taken the place of the religious leader as someone to turn to for psychological support and help (Halmos 1965).

From a consideration of the research literature around the use of spiritual interventions in therapy (e.g. Payne *etal*. 1992, Richards and Bergin 1997) it is apparent that the research so far has mostly focused on choosing a particular intervention and testing out its apparent effectiveness with a group of clients – for example, Propst *et al.* 1992. What is lacking are studies into what spiritual interventions actually are, when they are being used and in what way, how well received and how well valued by the client.

Forgiveness is probably the most commonly used and certainly the most researched spiritual interventions used in therapy and pastoral care. Prayer has also been a focus of a number of studies around its use in counselling (Rose 1993, 1996, West 1998b, 2000a, Gubi 2000). Richards and Bergin (1997) put forward and discuss at length a comprehensive list of possible spiritual interventions backed up by research studies as listed in Chapter 5. I have discussed in relation to the British context and have summarised (West 2000a) as:

- encouraging of forgiveness;
- prayer;
- discussing theological concepts and making references to scriptures;
- using spiritual relaxation and imagery techniques;
- helping clients live congruently with their religious values;
- self-disclosing spiritual beliefs or experiences;
- consulting with religious leaders;
- using religious bibliotherapy.

Two further interventions that can be added to this list are:

- asking religious questions during assessment;
- use of intuition/inspiration.

Although there are difficulties in defining 'spirituality' and distinguishing it from 'religion' (Richards and Bergin 1997), it is possible to define 'spiritual interventions' in therapy and pastoral care in terms of the list above and to be specific about what each intervention consist of. This wide range of possible spiritual interventions can, and should, open up our eyes to what can happen or be facilitated within the therapeutic encounter for the spiritually minded client.

We need to bear in mind in this context how David Hay discovered that 76 per cent of people admitted to have a spiritual experience but also their timidity in discussing their spirituality until they felt sufficiently safe. It poses the question: are therapy clients willing and safe enough to discuss and explore their spirituality. This is currently a matter of research by Chris Jenkins who has recently written (Jenkins 2003) of a client who found an unhelpful evangelical response from her first counsellor as she spoke of her spiritual issues and her second counsellor launched into a diatribe against Christianity in response to her client material. This neatly illustrates the counter-transference problems that when unexplored cause counsellors to act inappropriately and I would argue unethically in relation to their client's spirituality.

Having carried out a research project into forgiveness (Purcell-Lee and West 2000, West 2001a) I will focus on it in the next section as an example of a spiritual intervention in therapy. I will first explore the relevant literature in some detail before sharing the key themes and recommendations for practice arising from this research.

Forgiveness

Forgiveness is the name of love practiced among people who love poorly. The hard truth is that all of us love poorly. We need to forgive and be forgiven every day, every hour-unceasingly. That is the great work of love among the fellowship of the weak that is the human family.

Henri Nouwen

Although forgiveness remains a subject of some controversy and debate within the world of therapy it has been a regular feature of Christianity and other religions. In 1999 I directed a one-year qualitative research project into the use of forgiveness in therapy and pastoral care (Purcell-Lee and West 2000a, West 2001). In many ways the use of forgiveness could be taken as a case study into the potential of using spiritual interventions within counselling and psychotherapy.

Forgiveness is a key component of pastoral care (Jeff 1987, Leech 1994, Lyall 1995). Indeed Leech (1994) a Church of England minister writing on soul care insists that confession and forgiveness lie at the very heart of the Christian experience. Indeed we find that 'In principle, mainline Protestant beliefs place great emphasis on the power of God's grace and forgiveness' (McCullough *et al.* 2000 p. 122).

Forgiveness is a key feature of Christianity and it is explicitly addressed in many other religious traditions including Judaism, Islam and Hinduism (Rye *et al.* 2000). In Judaism in the Amidah, the sixth of the nineteen blessings used in the synagogue service begins, 'Forgive us, our father, for we have missed the mark' (quoted in Dorff 1998 p. 30). Indeed 'all the theistic world religions teach that people should forgive those who have harmed or offended them and seek forgiveness for wrong doings' (Richards and Bergin 1997 p. 212). In addition, in recent years we have seen the secular emergence of forgiveness expressed through popular self-help books on managing shame, guilt, grief, depression and non-religious uses of forgiveness by health professionals (Thoresen *et al.* 1998).

Even though forgiveness has been increasingly explored as an element in counselling and psychotherapy, especially in the USA (Richards and Bergin 1997, 2000) the models generated have had little impact on research and practice so far (McCullough and Worthington 1994). Arguably one of the key limitations of the largely secular practice of counselling and psychotherapy is their lack of recognition of the key role of forgiveness in psychological healing. Richards and Bergin (1997) drawing on their own and other research suggest that this consists of: (a) positive changes in affective well-being, (b) improvements in physical and mental health, (c) restoration of a sense of personal power, (d) reconciliation between the offended and the offender.

However, it is not an easy psychological or religious task to accomplish: 'Learning to forgive someone who has hurt you may be one of life's most demanding, yet meaningful, tasks' (Thoresen *et al.* 1998 p. 164). Despite the truth of this statement we find that within the USA forgiveness is not generally taught as a coping skill within education: 'children and youth are almost never provided the basics of forgiveness as a coping skill' (Thoresen *et al.* 1998 p. 185). Indeed this whole issue of how we acquire the ability to forgive remains a key research question: 'The question of how people learn to forgive is among the most important in the social sciences' (Enright and Coyle 1998 p. 139).

There is a danger that those involved in therapeutic or pastoral work that does include forgiveness may prematurely guide their clients towards forgiving others (Richards and Bergin 1997, Enright and Coyle 1998). 'The one-hour forgiveness intervention is an oxymoron for healing long-lasting, deep-seated injustices and for substantially reducing psychological symptoms of a clinical nature' (Enright and Coyle 1998 p. 157). There is an opposite danger, I believe, of the reluctance of some therapists to engage in forgiveness therapeutic work with religiously minded clients.

Enright and Coyle (1998) in seeking to define forgiveness insist that forgiveness is an interpersonal process, and that in genuine forgiveness, one who has suffered an unjust injury chooses to abandon his or her right to resentment and retaliation, and instead offers mercy to the offender. They make the following points:

- the injured one is able to recognise an actual injustice;
- the injured one chooses willingly and without coercion to respond with mercy rather than what could be justifiable retribution;
- forgiveness is decidedly moral, concerned with the good of human interaction.

In this way they suggest forgiveness can perhaps be distinguished from pardoning, condoning, excusing, forgetting and denying. They see forgiveness as voluntary and unconditional.

Enright (1996) suggests that we examine forgiveness in three aspects: forgiving others, forgiving self and seeking forgiveness. With colleagues (Enright and Coyle 1998) he has developed a 20-step process model of forgiveness that has cognitive, behavioural and affective phases that can be summarised in four major phases uncovering, decision, work and deepening. They refer to four published studies – with elderly females, college students, female incest survivors, and males whose partners had abortions – in which this model was applied. They conclude that these four studies taken as a whole, 'suggest that forgiveness may be taught and learned and that the outcomes can be quite favourable' (Enright and Coyle 1998 p. 154).

In contrast to Enright's model, Worthington (1998) regards forgiveness as a motivational experience based on developing empathy and has developed a five-step REACH model:

1   Recall the hurt;
2   Empathise with the one who hurt you;
3   (offer the) Altruistic gift of forgiveness;
4   (make a) Commitment to forgive;
5   Hold onto the forgiveness.

Two studies using this model that both show encouraging results are discussed in Thoresen *et al.* (1998).

Recent research has indicated that the frequency of use of forgiveness may correlate with the spiritual beliefs of the therapist
involved (DiBlascio and Proctor 1993). Indeed they found that
therapists' religious beliefs were weakly or completely unrelated to
their attitudes about the importance and usefulness of forgiveness
in therapy. However, we know from other research into the use of
spiritual intervention in therapy that lack of religious faith of the
therapist involved does not prevent them working effectively with
spiritual interventions with religiously minded clients (Payne et al.
1992, who present a useful summary of research into the use of
spiritual interventions in therapy).

From a practitioner perspective, Jacobs (1991) draws our attention
to the possibility of a shadow side to forgiveness: 'Forgiveness,
acceptance, and the generosity of care can be very powerful means
of exerting a hold or pressure over another person, especially if we
do let the other forget what we have done for them, nor how selfless
we have apparently been. Forgiveness can be a type of revenge'
(p. 10). Jacobs (1991) relates a fascinating story of a client, whom he
calls Brenda, who took 'revenge' on her stepfather by treating him
exceptionally well when he was dying. There is not space here to
explore such constructive revenge in any detail or even the revenge
in its more destructive forms, but it is worth noting that some acts
of forgiveness may in fact be a form of constructive revenge.

This challenges to deal with the issue of revenge and the difficult
feelings that need to be faced before forgiveness becomes possible
is well illustrated by an experience described by Marie McNeice
(1996), a religious sister in Belfast. She vividly describes her
experience when a friend of hers, Joe, was murdered in front of his
wife and three young children, whilst on their way to church in
Belfast in 1987. She writes:

> Joe's wife pleaded for no retaliation and talked about forgiving
> those who had murdered him. She turned to God for consolation
> and guidance, while I struggled to contain my anger, even going
> so far as to fantasise about how I could kill Joe's murderers
> myself. This desire for revenge seemed to be in direct conflict
> with gospel values and threw me into fear, confusion and guilt.
> I questioned my faith, values and beliefs and experienced a gap
> between them and the feelings of anger and revenge surging
> within me. The scripture challenge to 'love your enemy' and 'turn
> the other cheek' left me guilty about having such thoughts. It was

as though in order to forgive I must turn away from everything I was feeling. A choice had to be made, to accept these feelings or to deny them, and I couldn't make it.

With hindsight my spirituality was somewhat less than integrated, but the experience did lead me to question whether 'turning the other cheek' necessarily meant denying feelings of anger and revenge – normal human emotions and responses. I came to the conclusion that, while forgiveness involves going beyond our feelings, it also means acknowledging and owning them, not covering them up or escaping into nicer and more acceptable ones in an effort perhaps to make them more respectable.

(McNeice 1996 p. 12)

She invites us to explore such difficult feelings as part of a healing process akin to bereavement with forgiveness as not just the first step but final target in an ongoing process of reconciliation that will involve integrating such turbulent feelings.

In our research study at Manchester University (Purcell-Lee and West 2000, 2001a) into the practitioners' view of the use of

TABLE 6.1   Main themes emerging from the Forgiveness Research Project

Counsellors	Spiritual Directors
Catharsis/abreaction/insight/healing	Christocentric/theistic injunction (penitents and sacrament of reconciliation)
Completing incomplete *Gestalten*, (unfinished business)	Self-acceptance IS forgiveness
Narrative reconstruction/story repair (coming to terms with one's history)	Past participle of the verb to forget
Internal object repair and relationship repair	Burying the past but not the consequences
Rogers' core conditions	A quality of mercy, acceptance and love
Mutative metaphor for therapy process	Shadow side of therapist/healer as charlatan seeking power
Buddhist concept of harmony/ disharmony	Greek admonition to know thyself (Gnosis?)
Hebrew concept of Teshtevah and inclusion	Prisoners: remorse, forgiveness, reparation
I–Thou/I–It relationship	I–Thou/I–It relationship

forgiveness in therapy and pastoral care relationships. Ten therapists and ten spiritual directors were interviewed about the use of forgiveness in their work with clients. Using a heuristic phenomenological approach (Moustakas 1990, 1994, West 1998b, 2001d), the key themes that emerged from both sets of practitioners are summarised in Table 6.1. It will be apparent that there is much overlap between the themes produced from these two groups despite a difference in languages.

Based on this research, we have developed the following guidelines (see Box) for the use of forgiveness in therapy with the key proviso that forgiveness should benefit the forgiver. These guidelines remain provisional and in need of further testing and research and the author would appreciate feedback from practitioners as to their usefulness.

Draft guidelines on the use of forgiveness in counselling and psychotherapy

1   Forgiveness is a key feature of most, if not all, religions and has been increasingly used in secular therapy settings and in self-help books and groups. True forgiveness has health benefits to the forgiver.

2   Forgiveness is a powerful technique that when used appropriately can be of great benefit to clients in therapy. However, it needs to be used in a sensitive way that reflects the therapeutic needs of the clients. Premature or clumsy attempts to introduce or even to force forgiveness on a reluctant client will prove to be less than helpful and may well have harmful effects on the client.

3   Forgiveness is a process rather than necessarily a one-off event and may need to be returned to many times as differing facets of the underlying issue are explored. This process may never end and indeed for some people may never start.

4   Timing around the use of forgiveness is crucial and an invitation to a client to consider forgiveness should be offered tentatively if at all. Indeed there may need to be many months or even years of therapy, before this point is reached depending on the therapeutic needs of the client.

5   Resentment, anger, hurt and fear need to be faced and explored before true forgiveness is possible.

6	Forgiveness is not the same as reconcilia~~tion but~~ might lead to it.
7	Forgiveness may involve empathy on the part ~~of~~ for those needing forgiveness.
8	Forgiveness should benefit the client whether the~~y are~~ ing to forgive others, forgive self, or seeking forg~~iveness.~~

Recently working with a spiritually minded client, I found that during one particular session she uttered, twice within a few minutes, the word 'forgiveness' and then took it back. I naturally drew her attention to what was happening and an important work then occurred both around her forgiving others and also around her own relationship with forgiveness including forgiving herself. This was definitely a deepening of a spiritually alive experience for her (and for me). She was showing me how in her private, and perhaps barely conscious to her world, forgiveness was real but also showing me how reluctant she was to speak of this to another and maybe even admit it to herself.

Forgiveness has become something of a dirty word to secular therapists who recount stories of Christian clients pressurised to forgive their abusers before having sufficient opportunity to work through the abuse therapeutically. Our guidelines above address this issue and highlight how appropriate forgiveness is good for the forgiver too. However, the use of forgiveness and other forms of spiritual interventions in therapy remains an area of some controversy and of increasing research and practitioner interest especially in the USA. With clients' spiritual and religious beliefs remaining important to them, however challenging they may be to the therapeutic practitioner, it remains essential indeed ethical for the therapist to work effectively within their clients' belief systems. The therapeutic use of forgiveness holds great promise to aid the effective healing of many clients, and therapists need to inform themselves of how best to use it within their clinical practices.

Bereavement

For many of us spirituality is naturally part of the process of bereavement, a point of view echoed by many therapists working with bereavement, whom I have spoken to over the years. Occasionally I will meet a therapist who maintains that none of her/his clients

√ ᴧen bereaved have mentioned spirituality. This leaves me puzzling as to what the therapist meant by her/his use of the word 'spirituality' and also wondering how this therapist prevented her/his clients addressing issues related to spirituality. As in other aspects of our therapy work our counter-transference responses can have a huge impact on how our clients make use of the therapeutic space. To further explore the question of spirituality and bereavement I will present a few case vignettes including my own experiences to raise relevant issues.

Not long after the loss by suicide of a best friend, a middle-aged educated white man was walking in the grounds of a ruined abbey near his home where he had often walked with his friend. He felt a tangible presence of his friend near the ruined altar. He later had a vivid dream of his friend who was now living in a new flat and very content. They talked, were at ease, and it felt like an ordinary social occasion in many ways reminiscent of other good times they had shared together. The man spoke of his friend's father and their difficulties and became aware in the dream that his friend was in fact dead and immediately woke up and wept bitter tears. He was left feeling that both the 'presence' in the abbey and the dream encounter were real experiences and pointed him towards ideas about survival after death. He recognised that these experiences could be projections, expressions of his deep need to be in touch with his friend, and the processing of unresolved emotions about his friend. He also found that there were few opportunities to easily talk such experiences, that it was a taboo topic, that he might be considered mad.

A Gestalt psychotherapist Richard told me in a research interview: 'On some occasions, particularly when working with bereavement, I noticed that an almost tangible third presence sometimes comes into the room, maybe the spirit, the mark of the lost person. That's happened on a few occasions, and occasionally a presence can be felt that isn't human, that is maybe more divine, spiritual sort of thing.' If this presence in the therapy room was the person the client had lost, Richard 'would consider that an ideal time to invite the client to talk to such a person. Usually they would engage in a very contactful kind of dialogue. Occasionally the client decides that they are not ready, but normally it's a good sign that it's a good time for dialogue with the lost person. Occasionally it's God or a divine sort of presence that turns up. I often invite people to dialogue with God'. Richard has clearly reached a relaxed position in regard to such experiences and is able to integrate them into effective therapeutic work with his clients and he has appropriate supervision for this work.

A young woman lost a longed-for baby at 17 weeks. Her partner, a young man, cared for her as she experienced the grief and he felt that her will to live hung by a thread. After two weeks she seemed to have turned a corner and he went out to watch a film alone. During the film the hero rescued a young teenage girl. This triggered a bout of deep grief in the man as the lost baby was reckoned to be a girl and he felt unable to look after her, now she was dead. He felt he was therefore inadequate to her as a father since it was a father's duty to protect his children. He rang a close male friend and found some comfort in identifying who of his and his partner's dead relatives were now looking after the dead baby. He and his partner deeply regret not having been given the opportunity to view the dead child. A therapist friend of his told him he needed to let go of the baby, to allow her to move on but he protested with angry tears that he had never actually had the baby in his arms so how could he possibly let her go? The baby had been conceived on holiday when they had visited several sacred sites. The man went back there to experience his grief and became a member of the trust that looked after the sites.

A middle-aged man dreamt of his dead mother a few weeks after her death. In the dream she was now living in some kind of religious community where she had been given tasks to do and she showed off her accomplishments to her son. She then invited him to view her new flat. There was a wooden ladder up to a hole in the ceiling that led into her flat. Some of the rungs were missing. Desperately trying to climb up this ladder the man awoke to find himself making climbing movements. He wept bitterly at re-experiencing his loss but was consoled by the feeling of rightness about the dream, taking it to be a real encounter.

A few weeks after the death of my mother 11 years ago I was once more in the depth of the silence of a Quaker meeting desperately trying to make sense of her death. I then let go of the effort and I dropped down deeper into a quiet, calm, joyful familiar space in which I was out of my ordinary consciousness. Times passed and the experience faded and I returned to ordinary consciousness. I still had the same unanswered maybe unanswerable questions but realised that the place I went to and the experience I had there caused these questions not to matter at least not in that moment. They had less of a hold over me, the experience taught me that all will be well in some manner I do not really understand but I could have faith in and experience of.

All of these examples described above involve deep spiritual issues for me. There are other ways of construing these matters. For example, a psychodynamic interpretation of the projection of the loved one but I find this a poor reflection on the depth of the experience. However, my own first training was as a scientist who insists that we do not have the evidence to settle these matters. The mystic in me *knows* differently. The therapist in me insists that we honour the client's experience however bizarre, that we take account at a very deep level of the client's culture and that we have to be so cautious in introducing any kind of interpretation, any kind of psychiatric or other labelling. Let us focus instead on what support a bereaved soul might need.

These experiences of feeling that one is in touch with a dead loved one are more common than many people realise. David Hay (Hay and Hunt 2000) found that 25 per cent of the people who responded to his survey had had such experiences.

Retreats

> Oh how important is discipline, community, prayer, silence, caring presence, simple listening, adoration, and deep, lasting faithful friendship. We all want it so much, and still the powers suggesting that all of that is fantasy are enormous. But we have to replace the battle for power with the battle to create space for the spirit.
>
> (Nouwen 1989 pp. 6–7)

I was recently asked to write a short piece on retreats (West 2001b) which I will include here in an edited form below since it conveys something of my sense of what a retreat is, and can be and hopefully will make clear their possible use to clients and others whose therapeutic journey has taken an explicitly spiritual turn and who feel a need to spend time away from the world developing and deepening their relationship with spirituality.

Retreat is a curious word to describe the spiritual processes that we hope will unfold during a time away from our usual surroundings. There is usually plenty of time to be alone and not much to do but to be with the opportunity of dropping deeper into ourselves, which for those of us who use theistic words and notions maybe where we encounter God within, or some echo of the Divine.

Retreats then are an act of faith, a trust in a spiritual process, a belief that in taking time out from our daily lives that we will experience a deeper sense of ourselves as spiritual beings and remember ourselves as living in a spirited universe in which we live and move and have our being. Such an act of faith underpins daily practices of prayer, contemplation, meditation or whatever so we can envisage retreats as an opportunity to build on these disciplines or for many of us to re-visit and re-engage with these practices.

Retreats are so important to me I wonder why I do them so infrequently but the same could be said for my intermittent life of prayer. Indeed I recognise a fear I have of having to progress too quickly down the spiritual pathway, the terror implicit in the words Christ used of, 'Not my will but thy will be done'. Of course my actual experience of retreats does not bear this fear out, it merely lurks there on the edge of my consciousness.

My actual experience of retreats involves times of quiet joy, bitter tears, times of emptiness and futility, and times of deep change. I keep an occasional spiritual diary. Part of an entry from October 2001 whilst on retreat reads:

> The biggest sin with me today is not having the courage or self belief to have done those things earlier in my life that I could have. Simply not being full of myself enough. I was not raised to be open to myself in that way...Rogerians will recognise the deep lack of self esteem and self worth expressed here. My imbibing of our Christian culture which mixes up the problem of dealing with narcissism with the issue of self worth.

My current preferred form of retreat is an individually guided retreat in which I meet with my spiritual director at the retreat centre and pour out what is on my mind and soul (that bit is often a mystery and it is usually the most crucial bit). She listens, hearing what I don't say, or don't say in words and responds immediately in some ways and also offers me something spiritual to sit with, wrestle with or ignore until we meet again later that day or the next day. I then pass the time until we next meet in silence. This can be an extraordinary time, it can be a restless empty time or it can be a mixture. I often need to walk or do some other physical activity in this time. Writing things down in my spiritual journal usually helps and these entries make surprising sense when I re-read them months and years later – often in preparation for another retreat.

I am also a very occasional and very novice retreat leader only able to do so by clutching at the straw that tells me that the Holy Spirit is the true retreat leader and true director by relying on my more considerable experiences as a counsellor and group facilitator. I lead retreats because I have to, that is, I feel impelled (called if you like) to do it from time to time. My key approach as co-retreat leader is to trust in the process of spiritual unfolding that I feel is waiting to happen to each of us, despite our fears. Silence seems to be a necessary part of this process, as does time for meeting with one of the retreat leaders and there seems to be much value to be had from having structures like shared meals and times to talk as well as times for silence. I feel that my role is often that of listener or witness or, dare I claim it as a man, that of (spiritual) midwife. Traditionally midwives would sit and wait trusting in the natural processes and intervening when and if necessary. I am wary of claiming such a talent but the role model does seem appropriate and is well discussed by Guenther (1992) who assures us, 'Both men and women can be sensitive midwives of the soul' (p. 89).

In preparation for a retreat I co-lead in Autumn 2000, my co-facilitator Richard Summers and I produced a leaflet from which the following is extracted which sums up for me what I hope a retreat can be about and reflects the influence of my years of counselling.

We will be using periods of communal and individual silence; sharing and personal guidance to facilitate an inner exploration of ourselves as spiritual beings. This requires a preparedness to be open to the experience of the flow of God in our being which can manifest in a variety of different ways. It is usually a liberating process, but can be painful as we encounter the things that have been blocks to our spiritual growth and awareness. We aim to provide a safe and supportive environment in which we can be open to the process of unfolding and express our joy and pain.

Being spiritual is not a process of acquiring knowledge, or reaching a goal and the weekend cannot offer a specific outcome. Its outcome lies in the process and all of us who participate in the retreat will contribute to this. We ask that you come prepared to participate fully in a personal and communal unfolding, but no-one will be asked to do more than feels right and comfortable for them.

Retreats then are at best a time of spiritual nourishment, a stopping of from, and a letting go of, our usual life and patterns of living to remember more deeply who we are and why we are here; followed by a return refreshed and spiritually re-inspired to our everyday life.

The context

People who need support with their issues involving spirituality can access it in a number of ways:

1   If they belong to a religious or spiritual group they can seek it from those known within such groups as being competent to deal with such matters. Such people may carry labels like: priests, spiritual leader, elder, spiritual director, soul friend.
2   If they do not belong to such a group, or wish to seek support outside of their group, they could seek it from those recognised by such groups as competent in soul matters, that is, as in 1. In such a case the relationship established will have a different context to it in the account of both parties involved not belonging to the same faith group. An increasing number of people seek this kind of support and a number of suitably competent people so make themselves available. The National Retreat Association provides referral to spiritual directors.
3   Another option is to seek such help from a therapist. Most referral lists of therapists contain little if any mention of spirituality, so those clients wanting a spiritually minded therapist will have to ask questions of their would-be therapists.

Since spirituality still remains a difficult topic for many people outside of New Age circles to talk about, the use of word of mouth for an appropriate referral may not be available to the client seeking such help. In addition the difficulties around language discussed in Chapter 5 makes the selection of an appropriate therapist or helper that much harder.

The position is likely made worse by some of the actions of the evangelicals or fundamentalists sadly to be found within most religious groups in which the holy book is offered as *the* solution to all human problems. Religion-based therapy in such a context is truly a distortion of healthy therapy.

However, the insensitivity shown by too many secular therapists does not give me confidence that therapeutic encounter will always be a safe and appropriate place for the kind of careful working with spiritual issues that many of us need to engage in. The world of secular therapy has still to show us that it can honour and respect the clients' spiritual beliefs, experiences, practices and explorations. There is reason for hope; the therapy world is changing, reflecting changes in the wider world. In the next chapter I will be exploring how to research spirituality before the final chapter in which I will indicate an agenda for change to take this process forward.

Chapter 7

Researching Spirituality and Therapy

> The contribution of qualitative research lies in its capacity to approach research topics from a perspective of openness to different voices, a willingness to examine the historical 'archaeology' of therapeutic knowledge and an ability to deconstruct therapeutic language.
>
> (McLeod 2001a p. 18)

> Whoever wants to know about the human soul will learn nothing, or almost nothing, from experimental psychology.
>
> (Jung quoted in Ellenberger 1970 p. 694)

This chapter begins with the dilemma of how to actually research therapy and spirituality – how to systematically explore therapy and spirituality whilst remaining true to the territory and to the human beings involved. It also considers how to ask the awkward, the obvious and the naïve questions before arguing strongly for inner data analysis as part of a process of remaining spiritually alive in research. Throughout this chapter I will illustrate my argument with examples from my own and other's research into the realm of spirituality and therapy showing that such research is possible and valuable results can follow however difficult it might prove to be.

To research therapy and spirituality within the spirit of this book is no easy task. Traditionally research has relied on the separation of the researcher from that or those she/he researches. Great attempts are made when traditional research focuses on people to minimise, if not eliminate, the impact of the researcher on those researched. Such an approach is seen as 'objective' and 'scientific'. However, this is a 19th-century outdated view of science. Regretably, as Carl Rogers noted, modern psychology has tended and still tends to follow the same route: 'We have failed dismally to heed Robert Oppenheimer's (1956) warning, addressed to the APA when he pointed out that the worse thing psychology might do would be to "model itself after a physics which is not there anymore, which has been outdated".' (Rogers in Kirschenbaum and Henderson 1990a p. 358).

However, we are now in the 21st century in the post-Newtonian universe of quantum physics in which the observer affects the sub-atomic 'particles' by the simple act of viewing them. In addition there are instances of 'particles' effecting change in one another at a distance by no obvious causal route in a manner akin to Jung's synchronicity.

Apart from the difficulties already mentioned which apply to all research with or on human beings, the whole area of researching spirituality has its own special difficulties. These include:

1   What spirituality actually is, given that some people deny its existence, some feel the whole of life is intrinsically spiritual, some reserve spiritually for special moments or higher states of human development or both. Some see spirituality as definitely about things outside of themselves whilst others insist that no outside agency needs to be involved in human spirituality. In my own higher spiritual moments I have no clear sense of where I end and the rest of the universe begins.

2   For many of us how highest sense of spirituality involves spiritual experiences and spiritual states in which we are not in our usual state of consciousness and in which we are out of our minds. It is then so difficult to return from such a state with a clear appreciation of what happened – it is rather like trying to hold water in one's hands, to then try and put the experience into words represents another loss and potential distortion of the original experience, and finally to listen to the words used rather than sharing the actual experience is another loss or distortion for the hearer or reader of such words.

3   Finally there are those who would deny the validity of spirituality and spiritual experiences or regard them as worthless or even less than worthless ('mad', 'psychotic'). Rather than to stay caught up in that endless argument it makes sense to regard spirituality and spiritual experiences as human phenomena

of great importance to a huge number of people and thereby worthy of study. If David Hay's latest survey (Hay and Hunt 2000) is accepted then 76 per cent of the population have had spiritual experiences which suggests that these are in fact the norm and may well have a biological origin that Hay maintains following the lead of Hardy (Hay 1982, Hay and Hunt 2002).

These three points represent a strong argument for a qualitative phenomenological approach to researching spirituality although there has been much valuable quantitative studies done, for example, the work of David Hay (Hay and Morisy 1978, Hay 1982) and the various studies of the religious views of, and attitudes to, mystical experiences of US therapists (Bergin and Jansen 1990, Allman *et al.* 1992).

A number of qualitative methodologies have been developed in recent years which are comfortable with non-statistical forms of research and data analysis which at the very least tolerate the observer being in the field of research and in some cases capitalise on it. Several examples of such methodologies have been used within therapy and spirituality research including grounded theory, human inquiry groups and heuristics which will be explored below.

Grounded theory

A grounded theory is one that is inductively derived from the study of the phenomenon it represents.

(Strauss and Corbin 1990 p. 23)

Grounded theory remains the qualitative methodology of choice for many counselling and psychotherapy researchers. This despite the difficulties associated with what it actually is and how to do it. Its very popularity has tended to keep other qualitative approaches under-explored and under-utilised.

Grounded theory is a key form of qualitative methodology that has been successfully used in a number of research projects in the therapy fields (e.g. Angus and Rennie 1988, Rennie 1992, Bolger 1999, Mackay *et al.* 2001) and also in relation to spirituality (West 1997, Gubi 2000). McLeod (2001a) refers to grounded theory as the 'market leader' in qualitative research. In a recent issue of Psychotherapy Research (Vol 9(3) 1999), dedicated to qualitative research, three out of the eight research studies used grounded theory, and a search on Psyclit revealed 122 papers on grounded theory since 1993.

Grounded theory is a term coined by Glaser and Strauss (Glaser and Strauss 1967, Strauss and Corbin 1990) to describe a form of data analysis and theory development. The theory is developed from a systematic analysis of the data, rather than by formulating a hypothesis that is then tested. The unfolding theory is referred back to the data to ensure that it remains grounded in the data.

Unlike the analysis of quantitative data where one is testing the relationship between variables, in grounded theory analysis we are looking for categories and the relationship between them. It is thus a non-mathematical qualitative form of analysis, and the emergent theory is grounded in the empirical reality reflected by the data.

The grounded theory approach aims never to take anything for granted in analysing the data. It is keen to find examples of differences, things that do not fit since: 'following through on these differences adds density and variation to our theory' (Strauss and Corbin 1990 p. 109). However, this search for a dense theory that is grounded in the data is something that must finally remain incomplete: 'In developing a grounded theory we are trying to capture as much of the complexity and movement in the real world as possible, while knowing we are never able to grasp all of it' (Strauss and Corbin 1990 p. 111).

Briefly, data analysis is done in grounded theory by dividing the data up into what are called meaning units which may vary in size from half a sentence to several sentences which can stand alone. The first unit is put in a category with a provisional name to it. The second unit is compared with the first and if sufficiently similar is put into the same category, otherwise a new category is named. When a category contains six items a definition is given to that category. Eventually almost all meaning units are assigned categories that are defined. The categories are then placed into relationship with one another and a higher order model in which categories are composed of sub-categories and finally a core category is selected around which the model is constructed. In theory another researcher when given the same data would construct the same model.

As an example of breaking interview data down into meaning units, consider the opening comments made by one of my respondents who took part in my research into Quakers who were therapists (West 1998a). She is replying to my opening question 'May be the first place to start, if you could tell me something about your spiritual background':

> Yes, I came from an Anglican background with parents who'd both been missionaries. They'd come back to this country when I was born. But I often think of it now as I had a surfeit of religion. And in my teens I became very unhappy in the Anglican world and I think there was a time when my parents almost lived in and out of an evangelical approach, and I found that extremely difficult. And then I went to university in L and in fact had a real breakdown.

First Meaning Unit   Anglican background with both parents who'd been missionaries.
Second   They'd come back to this country when I was born.
Third   I had a surfeit of religion.
Fourth   In my teens became very unhappy in the Anglican world.
Fifth   There was a time when my parents almost lived in and out of an evangelical approach and I found that very difficult.
Sixth   I went away to university in L and in fact had a real breakdown.

One developing category is that of parents, religious background (Units 1, 5); another is her attitude to Anglicanism (Units 3–5); another one will relate to her mental health (Unit 6). Unit 2 currently does not suggest a category but it could be geography or home if more units occur that fit such a category.

As described above gradually sub-categories emerge and then categories of sub-categories. As an example of this I include in Table 7.1 the sub-categories from the second grounded theory I did from my researches into therapy and healing (full details in West 1995a, 1997). A pictorial representation how these categories and sub-categories can be grouped together is shown later in Figure 7.1.

However, having described grounded theory and shown how to begin an analysis we have to acknowledge a problem that its inventors fell out and that there are now at least two versions – that

TABLE 7.1   Grounded theory analysis 2 from research into therapy and healing

Sub-category		Brief definition of sub-category	
The Healing Process			
1	The healing relationship	1	How practitioner perceives the healing relationship
2	Context for incidental healing	2	Factors which contribute to incidental healing
3	Deliberate healing techniques	3	Examples of deliberate healing techniques used by practitioners
4	Enhancing therapy with healing	4	Ways in which deliberate use of healing techniques can enhance the process of therapy
5	Perceptions of therapy/ healing	5	How both client and practitioner regard therapy/healing
Practitioner Development			
1	Inspiration	1	The way respondents experience, understand and use inspiration
2	Therapy/healing as a vocation	2	The sense of vocation experienced by therapist/healers
3	Career background	3	Respondents' working background and how they became professional therapists
4	Therapist development	4	Personal therapy/healing training as a part of counsellor development
Experiences of Healers			
1	Creative initiatory illness	1	Dramatic illness preceding healer emergence
2	Contact with a healer	2	The role played by contact with healers in practitioner becoming a healer
3	Isolation/loneliness	3	Need to belong to a professional organisation of healers
4	Psychic experiences	4	Synchronous and psychic experiences that happen to healers

Spirituality

1	Religious background	1	Childhood experiences of organised religion
2	Practitioner's spirituality	2	Practitioner's current spiritual practices and their sense of the divine in their work
3	Impact of therapist's spirituality	3	How the therapist's spiritual development affects their work
4	Spirit presences	4	Practitioner's experience of spirit presences in their work
5	Working on spiritual issues	5	Examples of how practitioners work with their clients' spiritual issues

Dilemmas

1	Language	1	The difficulties in finding a shared language for talking about spirituality and healing
2	Taboo about spirituality and healing	2	Practitioner's experience of the taboo around discussing spirituality and healing
3	Supervision	3	The importance of, and difficulties with, supervision of healing work
4	Interpretation of spiritual phenomena	4	Issues concerned with the interpretation of spirituality and spiritual phenomena

advocated by Strauss and Corbin (1990) and that advocated by Glaser (1992). (Indeed McLeod (2001a) suggests that there are four possibly five versions of grounded theory now in existence.) Glaser (1992) regarded Strauss and Corbin's (1990) book as 'misconceives our conceptions of grounded theory to an extreme degree, even destructive degree' (Glaser 1992 p. 1). Indeed he viewed their method as forcing the data to yield categories rather than allowing the categories to emerge from the data through the grounded theory analysis, and he attempted to have the book withdrawn from publication. Despite some highly regarded supporters (e.g. Morse 1994, Rennie 1998) Glaser's approach to grounded theory has received far less usage than that of Strauss and Corbin. Besides this disagreement between its founders, there

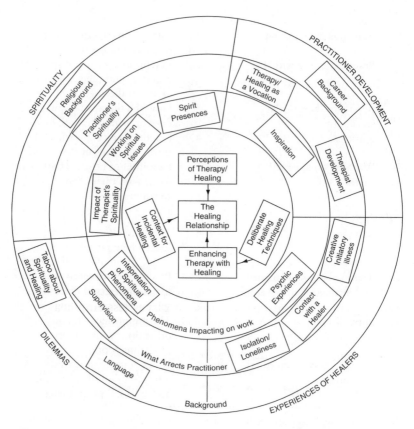

FIGURE 7.1   Pictorial representation of second grounded theory analysis

are a number of developments and refinements to grounded theory including that of Charmaz (2000) who presents a constructivist version of grounded theory and the approach adopted by Rennie (1998, 2000) that he calls 'methodological hermeneutics'. Rennie has been described by McLeod as 'stretching grounded theory' and 'who has perhaps taken grounded theory further than it was ever designed to go' (McLeod 2001a p. 89).

Given that grounded theory has been evolved and developed by its founders, by regular users like Rennie (2000) and by constructionists like Charmaz (2000), any comment on its limitations could be open to challenge. However, Charmaz (2000) informs us that the majority of grounded theory analyses are done from a positivist objectivist position which in Reason and Rowan's (1981) telling phrase are 'old paradigm' in that it is not rooted in collaborative and reflexive forms of research.

Grounded theory was developed in the 1960s to give qualitative research a more solid base from which to challenge a purely quantitative approach to research. Developed from a sociological viewpoint it assumes that data is collected by observation, interviewing and so on in a process in which the researcher is fairly inconspicuous. It assumed that there was an objective reality out there that could be viewed and analysed by following clearly defined rules of data collection and analysis. This quasi-scientific approach gives it its credibility, no bad thing, but there is a danger that it then anchors the research process in a non-reflective objectivist stance, that can lead, especially for those of us researching the world of therapy, to a denial of inter-subjectivity. Indeed Rennie, Phillips and Quartaro (1988) in discussing their choice of grounded theory for their research into the clients' experience of therapy choose it partially because 'it places less emphasis on the role of researcher in co-constructing the respondent's accounts' (1998 p. 140).

An example from my own research into psychotherapy and healing (West 1995a, 1997) well illustrates this issue. In the middle of a qualitative interview a metaphor occurred to me, that my interviewee was describing the transformation from being a therapist to also being a healer as like a butterfly emerging from a chrysalis. My interviewee responded to my metaphor with an enthusiastic 'Yes, that's it!' In a traditional grounded theory analysis with the focus on what people tell us, my metaphor should perhaps not be coded. Yet it felt like the metaphor could have been uttered by either of us; we were that closely that deeply engaged in exploring the topic, in a way akin to Buber's I/Thou relating.

In using grounded theory (West 1995a, 1997) I had a sense that something was lost in breaking down the data in relatively small units for coding, a feeling that some holistic totality was being broken down or lost, what has been called 'fracturing the data' (Charmaz 2000). Completing the grounded theory analysis resulted in a new totality emerging, but it is possible that this does not entirely reflect the original one.

In using grounded theory I was also troubled by its apparent assumption that knowledge could be best organised and represented in a hierarchical form of categories and sub-categories, a point explored by Charmaz (2000). Indeed in my study into therapy and healing I did two grounded theory analyses on part of my interview data and in the second analysis I was arranging my categories on my kitchen table which happened to be circular and I came up with a circular way of arranging my categories around one core or central category in bands that were interconnected and suggesting something of a mandala form, if in words, which seemed to convey more effectively and more visually the results of my analysis. Figure 7.1 included below shows this novel mandala-type form of grounded theory diagram that I produced on my kitchen table that puts the healing process at the heart of the analysis.

There is a deeper question here to be addressed and this is around how we view the world – that our data gathering especially about people is never value free and never objective. Data collection is socially constructed and a research report can be seen as a narrative, a form of storytelling built on explicit and implicit assumptions. If you hold that the world to be researched is outside of you and that you have no interconnection with it then you will not notice or you will tend to ignore or dismiss data that comes through such a connection. As already mentioned many grounded theory analyses assume that there is an objective truth waiting to be revealed and that another researcher given the same data will find the same truth. This is, I believe, as mistaken as those who objectify psychiatric diagnoses ignoring the changing fashions in diagnosis, however useful such diagnosis may prove to be.

Beyond Grounded theory: heuristics and human inquiry

Grounded theory is, as touched on above, open to 'stretching' and is a research tool that can be used creatively especially by those adopting a bricolage approach. Although grounded theory in its traditional form sought to minimise the impact of the researcher of those researched, there are other forms of qualitative research such as Moustakas' heuristics (Douglass and Moustakas 1985, Moustakas 1990, 1994, West 1998a,b) and Reason and Rowan's human or co-operative inquiry (Reason and Rowan 1981, Reason and Heron 1986, Reason 1988, 1994, Heron 1992, West 1996, 1998b) which turn this issue on its head. These approaches to research capitalise on the researcher's involvement with the research and use this involvement to aid the gathering of data and the forms of data analysis chosen. This has particular relevance for research into spirituality and therapy, given the difficulty in choosing where to stand in relation to spirituality.

To bring out the implications of a research approach that does capitalise on the researchers' involvement with those she or he researches, I will present Moustakas' heuristics and human inquiry in some detail before comparing and contrasting human inquiry, heuristics and grounded theory.

What is heuristics?

The power of heuristic inquiry lies in its potential for disclosing truth. Through exhaustive self-search, dialogue with others, and creative depictions of experience, a comprehensive knowledge is generated...Passionate yet disciplined commitment is vital.

(Douglass and Moustakas 1985 p. 40)

Moustakas then is not afraid of his involvement with those he is researching. Indeed, as will become apparent, his whole approach is based upon this. Such a view insists that it is through our very humanness that we can understand other humans. It has echoes of Carl Rogers who said 'the very feeling which has seemed to me most private, most personal, and hence most incomprehensible by others, has turned out to be an expression for which there is a resonance in many other people' (Kirschenbaum and Henderson 1990a p. 27). For Moustakas this means that the research process starts and ends with his inner being.

Moustakas is content with this being a subjective process. However, this is clearly a disciplined subjectivity: 'heuristic research is a search for the discovery of meaning and essence in significant human experience. It requires a subjective process of reflecting, exploring, sifting, and elucidating the nature of the phenomenon under investigation. Its ultimate purpose is to cast light on a focused problem, question or theme' (Douglass and Moustakas 1985 p. 40).

According to Moustakas (1990) there are six phases to heuristic research: initial engagement, immersion, incubation, illumination, explication and creative synthesis. However, although heuristic research does move through these phases, it is not necessarily a linear process and certainly does not constitute a rigid framework.

I have elsewhere explored the use of Moustakas' heuristics in my own research into therapists' spirituality (West 1998a,d), so will only briefly cover his stages here. The first phase of heuristic research is that of *initial engagement*. This involves a process of clarifying what it is we want to research. Moustakas suggest that we need to engage in self-dialogue about what we want to research. He regards it very much as a process of inner searching and that it is something that should not be hurried. He insists that if we stay with this process the research question will eventually emerge.

The second stage of heuristics is called *immersion*. This is the stage in which we have to really live the question, awake, asleep, and in our dream. We are asked to enter fully into life around the research question and we find synchronous occurrences, when opportunities arise in chance meetings with people to explore our research question. Moustakas tells us of how people, places, meetings, nature all offer us possible understanding of the phenomenon we are researching.

The next stage of the process is that of *incubation* in which the researcher retreats from the intense focus on the question and allows called, tacit, intuitive and often unconscious processing of the research to continue. This allows us to draw on what Polanyi (1962) called 'tacit knowledge', that we know more about a phenomenon than we usually allow ourselves to admit and access. As Douglass and Moustakas put it: 'to know, without awareness of how or why one knows, is the sine qua non of tacit knowing' (1985 p. 50). During this incubation it is important to put the research aside and get on with other tasks in one's life. Physical activities can be a great help such as gardening, walking or cycling. It is important to trust these tacit processes. At such a time it can feel like one has accumulated a mass of data but is unable to make any sense of it.

This is *illumination*, in which new awareness, new insights emerge resulting in a new synthesis. Moustakas insists that this is a natural process if one is open to tacit and intuitive knowledge. Qualities and themes relating to the question emerge into consciousness. However, this cannot be forced or strived for. Following from illumination comes the *explication* stage that is usually somewhat easier. In this stage the task is to fully examine what has emerged, teasing out layers of meaning. Moustakas suggests that we can make use of Gendlin's *Focusing* (1978) which is a way to systematically explore some inner insight. Certainly there needs to be a process akin to meditation of indwelling, self-searching, self-disclosure and reflexivity around the research process as a prelude to understanding what is shared.

The final stage is that of *creative synthesis*. This is where we meet the final challenge to pull all of the research together into some final form that does justice to it. Needless to say this is a tacit and intuitive process. Moustakas is keen that we use a narrative description using quotes and examples to truly convey the research process and findings. He openly advocates our use of poetry, storytelling, drawings and painting. Moustakas insists that for this final stage we need a deep knowledge of the data, solitude and time to meditate on the topic.

Some comments on the use of heuristics are appropriate here. The involvement of the researcher in the process yields valuable data. For instance, self-disclosure by researcher can facilitate trust and deeper levels of sharing of understandings of the phenomenon. There is the danger of collusion and of missing the obvious in such research but it provides access to material that an outsider would take a longer time and maybe never reach. Using heuristics we need to be mindful that we are collecting stories about phenomenon that have their own truth to participants. Finally, heuristics delivers findings that are usable and are congruent with the subtleties of psychotherapy and spirituality and are akin to the therapeutic process. (These points are further discussed in West 1998a.)

To illustrate this use of heuristics I will present the key findings from my qualitative study into 18 Quakers which sought to explore the impact of their spiritual faith on their work as psychotherapists and counsellors. It was that their faith did impact on their working and between 12 and 15 of the respondents agreed with the following statements:

1   My spiritual faith underpins all of my therapy work.
2   My spiritual faith gives me something extra when I am working (this can include being spiritually inspired, preparing spiritually before meeting clients and the use of prayer).
3   There is no conflict or distinction between my Quakerism and my therapy work.
4   The individual nature of the Quaker spiritual journey enables me to be open to my client's spiritual journey.

Just over half agreed with the statement 'I feel called or Spirit-led to work as a therapist'. Nearly three-quarters of the respondents agreed to the statement that they were inspired in a therapy session at times in a way similar to the Quaker experience of being inspired to speak during a Quaker Meeting for Worship. Four respondents had experienced some conflict between their faith and their therapy work that can occur with work colleagues or with supervisors. Clearly a heuristic approach did deliver valuable research data and was one way of creatively suing the involvement of the researcher with the research topic.

What is human inquiry?

> The essence of co-operative experiential inquiry (i.e. human inquiry) is an aware and self-critical movement between experience and reflection which goes through several cycles as ideas, practice, and experience are systematically honed and refined.
>
> (Reason 1988 p. 6)

A key feature of human or co-operative inquiry groups is that the details of what is researched and how it is researched are decided by the group rather than by the researcher alone. Human inquiry groups proceed through a process of cycling. The first stage involves group members gathering together to agree (or not as the case may be) on the nature and the methodology of the research and on the action to be taken. The second stage requires group members to engage in the research action, which may take place during group sessions or in group members' lives outside of the group. The third stage involves fully experiencing the action taken. This represents a stage of experiential knowing in which members are open to what is going on and 'bracket off' their preconceptions as much as possible. Finally group members reflect together on the research so far, including drawing conclusions and initiating further research cycles.

Human inquiry is a form of research *with* people, not *on* people, that is carried out co-operatively. It is research that is co-created. The researcher does not deny his or her involvement with the research process but capitalises on this involvement, indeed using this as another source of data and as information to guide the research process. Such informed involvement is called 'critical subjectivity' (Reason and Rowan 1981).

Human inquiry groups take a whole-person approach to research. This is reflected in its view that there are at least three different kinds of knowledge that can be acquired and explored during the human inquiry cycle: *experiential* knowledge gained through direct face-to-face encounter with people, places and things; *practical* knowledge gained through practice – knowing how to do something; and *propositional* knowledge – knowledge about something expressed in statements and theories (Reason 1994). John Heron (1998) has recently proposed a fourth type of knowledge presentational which he places between prepositional and experiential knowledge.

It will be apparent that such a form of researching involves the researcher not remaining in control of what is researched and how it is researched. My own research into therapy and healing (West 1995a, 1997) used a human inquiry group (West 1996) and John Heron has written extensively of his own use of human inquiry groups into what he calls 'sacred science' (Heron 1998). Although human inquiry is a collaborative form of research it is often difficult to deeply engage the participants in the research report-writing. Indeed, it can be argued that producing a report is not a necessary outcome, indeed why the big emphasis on intellectual knowledge (which Reason and Rowan refer to as propositional knowledge)?

The human inquiry group that formed part of my researches into therapy and healing decided to continue to meet after the data-gathering research phase was complete in June 1994.The group called itself the PsychoSpiritual Initiative (PSI) and has met three or four times a year for a weekend ever since. Initially it met as a kind of peer supervision group around therapy and healing for its members and then began to offer a consultative space for people with issues around therapy, healing and spirituality. Over 30 people have made one-off consultations with the PSI group since 1994 and it works spiritually and intuitively with all of its visitors (visitor being the name PSI chooses to call its consultees).

Inner data analysis

The challenge having researched in an interconnected way is how to analyse the data gathered in the same spirit. In Table 7.2, I summarise the three forms of qualitative research methodologies that I have discussed in this chapter so far and which have been applied,

TABLE 7.2   Inner data analysis

	Grounded theory	Human inquiry	Heuristics
View of research reality or field	Out there	Co-created	Co-created but understood within the researcher
Role of researcher	Detached participant observer	Actively engaged	Actively engaged including own internal processes
What is the data?	What the researcher sees and is told and collects from written documentation	All that and all those involved in the research experience about the phenomenon	Ideally all that those involved in the research experience about the phenomenon including the researcher's inner processes
Where does the understanding of the phenomenon lie?	With those researched excluding the researcher	With all those who took part in the research including the researcher	Ultimately within the researcher: inner or tacit knowing

as mentioned above, to therapy and spirituality research. As is already apparent they differ in their view of what is reality. For heuristics and human inquiry groups the reality that is explored in research is co-created by researcher and research participants and for research purposes is understood within the researcher. In contrast in traditional grounded theory, reality is objective and out there waiting to be researched. The implications this might have for therapy and spirituality research should be apparent.

Inevitably the role of the researcher in all three approaches reflects these differing views of reality. The researcher in grounded theory aims for some sort of detached or perhaps participant observation whilst in human inquiry and heuristics the researcher is actively and deeply engaged with the research topic. These basic differences are reflected in what is understood as the data: in grounded theory it consists of what can be collected in written form or by interviews and observations. In human inquiry it includes all that the group members including the researcher experience, in heuristics the data is extended to include some apprehension of inner processes of all those involved in the research including the researcher.

Finally there is the complex question of where the understanding of the phenomenon being researched lies. In grounded theory it comes from a study of the people researched and the data gathered; in human inquiry reality is seen as co-created by all of the group members. In heuristics Moustakas insists that it is to be found within the researcher and elucidated by an intuitive and tacit process of knowing.

This interconnectedness between the researcher and those researched mirrors the therapeutic relationship, indeed good qualitative researchers make use of empathy as do good therapists. This interconnectedness is also an aspect of many people's spirituality and spiritual experiences as discussed in Chapter 4.

Moustakas' heuristics stays with the research truth that it is the researcher who initiates the research, who is the one who passionately wants and needs to know and understand the phenomenon being researched. He offers us the bold strategy of not relying on logical systematised forms of data analysis that mimic quantitative research. For Moustakas the data analysis is done by an inner process that is intuitive and largely unconscious and is tacit knowing. That is, we know more than we usually allow ourselves to know and we can use this ability for data analysis. It is in fact not easy and demands the same immersion in the data which happens with all forms of qualitative research.

It requires great trust and courage to analyse data in this fashion, great trust not to fall back on the logical approach of, say, grounded theory that promises to deliver so much and to instead trust in our largely unconscious intuitive powers... but it delivers. It also is profoundly life changing. Good qualitative research is meant to empower those researched (McLeod 2003). It also changes the researcher, as Polanyi (1962) states: 'Having made a discovery, I shall never see the world again as before. My eyes have become different: I have made myself into a person seeing and thinking differently. I have crossed a gap, the heuristic gap, which lies between problem and solution' (p. 143).

This was clearly the case for me with my research into the impact of the spiritual beliefs of the Quaker therapists I interviewed. It led me to focus more fully on the role that spirituality plays in my therapy practice and in my teaching and in my life as a whole

(West 1998a). This fed into an unease about working within secular institutions that lack the ethical values I associate with spirituality (discussed in West 1998d).

Inner data analysis represents the way I approach spirituality and therapy research and I feel it does justice to the complexities of our interrelatedness and interconnectedness, something which bedevils modernist empirical research but which truly reflects the reality of psychotherapy and the lived spiritual life.

Philosophy matters

It could prove useful at this point to briefly touch on the philosophical stances underlying both grounded theory and heuristics. Just as the differing schools of counselling and psychotherapy have at their core differing views of what it is to be human and what constitutes effective therapy, differing qualitative methodologies are based on differing worldviews and what is considered appropriate and valuable data and data analysis. According to McLeod (2001a) all qualitative methodologies are either phenomenological (phenomenology strives to describe the essence of every day experience) hermeneutic (hermeneutics is concerned with the interpretation of texts) or a mixture of both. Moustakas originally insisted that heuristics was different to phenomenology 'Phenomenology ends with the essence of experience: heuristics retains the essence of the person in experience' (Douglass and Moustakas 1985 p. 43) but later (Moustakas 1994) came to regard heuristics as a branch of phenomenology. McLeod (2001a) maintains that grounded theory can best be considered as a varying mixture of both phenomenology and hermeneutics.

Not wishing to be a fool rushing in to places wise men and women fear to tread, it does strike me that we researchers need to adopt a research methodology that does not do violence to our deepest sense of what it is to be human (e.g. various research studies that deliberately mislead people). Beyond that how one poses the research question after much indwelling on it could lead to a pragmatic choice of methodology, as advocated by Patton (1990). My gut instinct tells me that there is a lot to be said for more than one methodology, if sufficient care is taken, whereby the several approaches are used to gain a fuller picture of the research area. Of course, a final pragmatic take may well be what is possible given the time and resources available and what the funders might welcome, and as a bottom line what will best inform counselling and psychotherapy practice? In the context of spirituality and therapy research, the appropriate use of more than one methodology might well give us a fuller picture of the phenomenon under consideration.

Bricolage

The report of such a research study may well resemble what Denzin and Lincoln called a 'bricolage': 'A complex, dense, reflexive, collagelike creation that represents the researcher's images, understandings, and interpretations of the world or phenomena under analysis' (1994 pp. 2–3). This is in response to a realisation that objective reality can be captured and only known through its representations. Hence, Denzin and Lincoln advocate the use of 'multiple methodological practices, empirical materials, perspectives, and observers... as a strategy that adds rigor, breadth, complexity, richness, and depth' (2000 p. 5). This is a logical stance for developing qualitative worldviews of differing realities explored by differing methodologies.

Of course this notion of 'bricolage' has itself been criticised and McLeod (2001a) has put forward the notion of a 'generic' approach to qualitative research that attempts to move beyond what could become a stale debate around methodologies. These arguments begin to resemble the pure schools of counselling and psychotherapy versus the integrative or eclectic approach debate, and ultimately have the same feeling of sterility. I am still left with the question from the start of this chapter how can we research spirituality in therapy in a way that does justice to our understandings and knowings of this complex human phenomenon.

Having presented several useful methodologies and the concept of the bricolage I remain fairly comfortable with Patton's (1990) pragmaticism of an informed following of my gut instinct explored during a process of deep contemplation, prayer and meditation! Interestingly David Rennie, one of the world's leading therapy researchers who has popularised the use of grounded theory now advocates choosing categories on the basis of what feels right in a paper entitled, 'It rises from my gut: embodied categorizing in grounded theory' (Rennie and Fergus 2001). As John McLeod reminds us: 'Good qualitative research does not derive from following a procedural recipe book... Good qualitative research is a matter of imagination, creativity, courage, personal integrity, empathy and commitment' (2001a p. 160). Finally, the findings of such research have to have a relevance to the practitioners and their clients. This book has been informed by much good research conducted in therapy and spirituality.

The culture of the researcher

I recently had the pleasure of doing some research with Mansor Abu Talib (West and Mansor 2002). I gave five randomly selected interview transcripts from the 18 I had carried out with therapists who were also Quakers during 1995–1996 (West 1998a). I asked Mansor to read through the transcripts and share his immediate reactions to them. I was aiming to access those reactions which we often blank out, or are unconscious or semi-conscious of, as we attempt to bracket them. Mansor decided to also do a data analysis. A paper based on our two analyses was recently published (West and Mansor 2002). More recently Janet Muse-Burke has done a similar analysis to Mansor's. I first supply some biographic information on all three of us in Table 7.3.

All three of us produced similar sub-themes which in my analysis (West 1998a) were presented as nine core themes, Mansor's analysis (Mansor 2002) yielded five and Janet's three. A key difference between my analysis and Mansor's was his category of higher levels which included 'soul searching' and 'doing God's work'. My own closeness to the respondents in terms of shared faith led me to categorise in terms of 'relationship with their spiritual faith' and 'sense of calling'.

In the table below I have included the commentaries by Mansor and by Janet in which they seek to capture their reactions to their data. I reflect on these commentaries in the third column of the table which led me to return to my research diary in order to illuminate my own reactions to the data.

TABLE 7.3   Biographic information on Quaker data analysers

	William West	Mansor Abu Talib	Janet Muse-Burke
Ethnic origin	White British	White Malaysian	White American
Religious affiliation	Quaker	Islamic	Baptist

Mansor Abu Talib	Janet Muse-Burke	William West

Soul searching: I found that most participants seemed to wrestle in search of something ... kind of finding a truth or hard evidence. There's an element of a vacant soul that stood empty and needed to be crammed with something good.
I wonder why that soul was unoccupied? And why they thought it need restructuring? Interestingly, self-exploration was daily ongoing, undertaking that they did and that itself seemed to have made them more spiritual.

I was chosen: I found that most participants felt that they were 'chosen' by GOD to become healers or counsellors or drawn to the helping profession. I am not sure about that! I think that sounds arrogant! In other words that means GOD chose me and not you! The argument is then 'Why did GOD choose you?'

However, I accept as true that our life scripts has been written ('azali') right when we

Calmness, quietness, and inner peace were emphasized as an important element of the meetings that were employed before, during, or after counseling work. It was, at times, described as "getting centered." This seems to be an important, though unique aspect of counseling work for Quakers. First, this experience of silence in the Quaker meetings seems unique. As a Baptist, I do not experience much silence in our church services. Rather, the time is mostly filled with singing, music, preaching, reading, and praying aloud. Likewise, I believe that the American culture does not value or appreciate silence.All of the counselors-in-training with whom I have worked through the seven years of my training have struggled with silence. Being comfortable with silence is a skill on which most students need to do intense work.

Another commonality I observed was the *belief that one should not*

I feel humbled by the depth of engagement made by Mansor and Janet in their wrestling with the data and by their willingness to be open and frank about their reactions to the transcripts. This is pure gold from a research point of view and is the kind of comment that is missing from most qualitative research studies even those which include a reflexive aspect.

It leads me to remember that a key reason for my doing this research was to find out if anyone had solved some of my dilemmas about how to be spiritual and how to be a counsellor! Looking back over my research diary and also the memos to myself that I often recorded immediately after an interview, I notice, in some of them, that as I struggle to make sense of what I am being told, there are echoes of my own inner debates on issues raised: "Some people seem to have the freedom to do what comes to hand and is useful, some don't.

Mansor Abu Talib	Janet Muse-Burke	William West

were first born, like some sort of fate. Being chosen meant being selected out of so many ... are those prisoners waiting to be prosecuted also being chosen? Being chosen also mean you are receiving mercy ('hidayah') from GOD as GOD knows what is best for you. Spirituality always evoked a sense of the presence of 'barakah', meaning 'grace' which flows in the universe and within the life of man to the extent that he dedicates himself to God. Therefore, I believe that the participants who claimed themselves as being 'chosen' must have experienced total dedication or surrender to GOD.

Apart from that, I also feel that participants regard themselves as better-off or at higher level of functioning. This is important in helping professionals, as we always have to be a step ahead as compared to our client.

I was doing GOD work: GOD is most able to do whatever he desires.

impose one's faith onto clients. For example, some of the interviewees contended that they use open language (e.g. "I'll think of you.") so as to not impose their religious faith on their clients. Within their context, that was a spiritual comment. However, within the context of the client, that may or may not have been a spiritual reference. Personally, this has been an important conflict for me. The Baptist faith emphasizes evangelism. In contrast, my counseling training has very much been anti-religion/anti-faith/anti-spirituality. Thus, I have been left with a strong, internal turmoil regarding how I can reconcile these two points of view. I have had to work this out for myself because I did not feel that there was anyone with whom I could discuss this conflict who was without bias or prejudice.

The *strength that the Quaker faith provides* to do the difficult work of counseling was also

Maybe recent trainees are more bounded/ more restrained by supervision? Is integration of therapy and spirituality possible? Without a new role (of helper) emerging – therapist as shaman/wise person/ spiritual director?"

"Jacob's [name changed] interview, he starts off very committed spiritually (working as a priest before becoming a Quaker) and then eventually finds his way into counselling. So that his spirituality is a kind of grounding to his counselling work. In contrast Frances matches a bit more to my experience of the counselling coming first and the spirituality comes in at a stage in the developing of the counsellor. So it is less clear and questions of how to fit spirituality and counselling together occur. This reflects a similar dilemma in my earlier research into integrating therapy and healing (West 1997) about how those who were healers before becoming counsellors

I am not sure, that as humans we can conceitedly claim that we are commissioned to do the job that GOD is doing. There's a kind of double meaning in this word which I myself repent of using. GOD does not have to go through another human being that he had created to get what is needed. I would rather say that as counsellor I am doing what GOD asks me to do, that is, to help another fellow human being, as it is a right thing to do. I will help you to my fullest ability with blessing of ALLAH.

Needless to say, the sentiment of being noble and doing the right things might promote the development of spiritual being in oneself. I believe the Rogerian principle that people are in the process of 'becoming' of being self-actualised to me includes being spiritual (not necessarily being religious). Islamic teaching encourages counselling. The Prophet Mohammed said: "Religion (Islam) is sincere counselling and good advice".

noted throughout the interviews. I believe that this belief fits very well with my viewpoint as a Baptist. From childhood, I viewed God as one on whom I could rely with my concerns, burdens, difficulties, and successes.

Also, the interviewees commonly described *a sense of being held by God* in counseling. They mentioned feeling a peace, warmth, lovingness, and calm about them. This also fits with my experience in counseling. Though I don't feel it a lot, there are special moments with clients in which I have felt God's presence guiding me through, helping me be an instrument of His grace.

Most of the interviewees noted that *spirituality and supervision don't mix*. I have also had this experience. In the United States, there is an emphasis on the separation of church and state. I believe that this value has been generalized to the point that faith is diminished in many respects. Likewise, the program

seemingly had an easier time of it... Jacob has got a sharing Quaker group, almost like a counselling group that's within a Quaker setting where the Quaker way of life is taken for granted and weaves in and out of the counselling. So in effect he's got a sort of psycho spiritual group which is lacking elsewhere. It may be (may be!) that some of us want to bring the spiritual into our work, because we don't have the satisfaction of working at all in that situation where the spiritual is taken for granted, not just taken for granted but given it head, welcomed and involved."

Talib's and Janet's commentaries show me how these research interviews would have likely taken a totally different direction with an outsider researcher, either non-counsellor and/or non-Quaker. A fair bit of the data would likely remain the same but some of the data would be different as the outsider struggled to make sense of this different world and culture.

Mansor Abu Talib	Janet Muse-Burke	William West
	in which I have trained seems to view religion and spirituality nega tively. As such, I have generally found that spirituality could not be safely discussed with supervisors. Lastly, it seemed that many interviewees did *not feel that they were called to counseling.* Perhaps this is related to the fact that most of them did not find their current faith until they were older and alreadyin the counseling profession. This contrasts sharply with my experience. I believe that the Baptist faith empha sizes "being called." Likewise, there is an emphasis on using one's spiritual gifts actively. As such, I have always felt that I was called to be a counselor and that God gave me these gifts to help provide psychological and spiritual help to others.	

Clearly what these extracts from Mansor's comments on these themes are indicating is his fairly strong and at times passionate reaction as a religious and Islamic man to statements made by the Quaker therapists in the interviews. He is making visible what most of us hide from view, either as researcher or as counsellor, namely our reactions to what we hear. This is a courageous and important sharing on his part. It leads me to wonder what my own reactions would be to similar interviews with Islamic counsellors done by him.

Janet's comments are equally revealing showing how her Baptist faith could connect to what she was reading in the interview transcripts and it raises interesting questions about cultural differences between the USA and Britain in relation to both therapy and religion.

I am currently receiving similar commentaries from a number of people from differing backgrounds from many parts of the world that will be analysed in the near future.

Thinking about these different analyses and comments on the interviews, I am reminded yet again of Heron (1992) telling us that totally bracketing (i.e. putting aside our presuppositions) is impossible. We are in the field when doing qualitative research and at best can aim for 'critical subjectivity' (Reason and Rowan 1981). This is a truth we cannot escape and, as in the therapy relationship, it colours everything. Denzin (1989) points out that 'genders filters knowledge', we can extend this to say 'self filters knowledge' or to frame it spiritually 'soul filters knowledge'.

I think that there is always the possibility that we research ourselves in others or in our projections onto others. Checking out our findings with our respondents helps minimise this as does dialogue with the wider audience for our research. My feeling is that we never get enough of this and so our findings inevitably remain provisional.

This research has profound implications given the commonly stated view that different researchers using the same qualitative research method should arrive at a more or less identical analysis. It could be argued that the three researchers in this case used different methodologies – heuristic and thematic analysis. However from the commentary and discussion it seems clear that the difference in the data analysis has more to do with culture differences than methodological differences.

There are a number of implications that can be deduced from this research, which include:

1   The researcher is always operating in cultural context, that is, the researcher is always present in the research as a total and cultured being in the context of the research. Attempts at bracketing does not substantially change this.

2   The researcher is unique: Suppose we had a fourth researcher who was female, non-religious, an engineer, or 2nd generation British Muslim and so on, how would the analysis and commentary then change? Does anyone really believe that giving the same data to another person with the same instructions to analyse can necessarily result in an identical analysis?

3   What do words mean? How far can we assume we know what somebody means when they use a word we are familiar with, especially if we are in different cultures or sub-cultures? For example the word 'wicked' has a totally different meaning to British youth than it does for Christian fundamentalists. This is also especially clear in the differing understandings of what the word 'spiritual' means to the researchers. My view in reflecting on spirituality in modern Britain is that many people now regard spirituality as something they experience experientially and that this may or may not be contained by traditional religious frameworks.

4   For Mansor there is little separation between spiritual and religious. For Janet there is the pain of her spirituality not being accepted within her training as a counselling psychologist.

5   All of the above points apply to therapy, namely that the therapy has a culture, is unique, and has a particular cultural way of understanding what words mean.

6   How much is qualitative research (as is therapy) as we understand it and practise it – white, western, middle class and post-modern?

7   The therapist's valuing of, and listening to, the uniqueness of the individual within their cultural and sub-cultural context is an important element to carry over into qualitative research. However, just as the therapist's approach will be underpinned by their culture and sub-culture so will the researcher's. This guides and shapes what research questions get asked and how they are understood.

Conclusion

This chapter has explored the complex question of how to research spirituality and therapy that has many of the same dilemmas involved in researching people but a few extra ones added in because of the nature of spirituality. I have drawn on my own experiences of engaging with these issues over the last ten years to illuminate and not so much offer solutions more to indicate ways of approaching this topic. There is something most satisfying for me in the recognition that spirituality and therapy can not be objectified, that we cannot detach ourselves from the data in any useful way however much we might wish to. This to me is the essence of the human condition – imperfect, messy, engaged, painful, hard work at times and just occasionally graceful and glorious.

Chapter 8
Soul Attending

In this final chapter I seek to re-visit the main themes of this book relating to psychospiritual practice and point us towards the new type of psychospiritual practitioner that I feel is now emerging. Some elements of this practice are explored in what follows in terms of language, soul attending, spiritual self care, appropriate supervision, courage, ethics, necessary knowledge, and an agenda for change. Finally I speculate somewhat about future possibilities.

Language

I have introduced and made frequent use of the term 'psychospiritual' in this book to describe ways of psychotherapeutically working with clients that is inclusive of spirituality. I wondered about using the word 'spiritopsyche' but felt that this word implies that the pastoral care or spiritual direction frame is the key one and so somewhat reluctantly (as I do like the sound and feel of this word) I will stick to the word 'psychospiritual'. Further developments that are needed is in the area of vocabulary and concepts that do justice to spirituality and religion as practised in differing cultures and sub-cultures on our planet. This is why Wilber's attempt to create a universal model of human spiritual development is so important, why the study of traditional healing approaches like shamanism and spiritual healing are crucial, and finally why the various ways that interfaith dialogues are developing should be welcomed. However, we do need to remember that many people's spirituality in Britain is not contained within existing religions.

It is also important that our exploring and theorising are not contained within our various schools of therapy. There is a whole area of discussion of spiritual issues in non-spiritual terms that is also worthy of respect. Indeed it feels at times as if we do need a fair measure of translation between differing schools of therapy and differing religious and spiritual traditions. All of this might seem like a tall order for us (therapists) to face but our clients deserve no less than our proper respect for their spiritual and religious beliefs and experiences.

Soul attending?

I am currently wrestling with the label 'counsellor' having in the past used the label 'therapist'. I choose the label counsellor since I felt it was a low key and less medically and psychiatrically linked word than psychotherapist, and also a more humble word. As my work evolved in recent years and became more explicitly spiritual it became necessary to include the word spiritual in description of my practice, and my clients since that time have responded well to this word.

Counselling has moved on becoming increasingly professionalised and my own practice has evolved and developed and I find that the word counsellor is harder to lay claim to and to own. I wonder if this change in me reflects similar changes in others? My musings on these matters led me to review my own development as a practitioner. I recall evolving out of a pure-school approach in the mid-1980s. (I was quite purist, almost fundamentalist at first for at least 18 months, I felt that my school had the answer for life, the universe, every problem!) I gradually valued other approaches to therapy, similarly other religions and paths to spirituality and cultures in general (including traditional healing practices from other cultures and my own). Inevitably I found myself in a different place, in a different relationship to therapy itself and to spirituality.

In my pursuit of the therapeutic encounter in a context that is spiritual I have asked myself on a number of occasions: should I retrain as a transpersonal therapist? Whilst this would likely improve my therapeutic practice, my contact with transpersonal therapists and writers so far does not lead me to feel that such a training would resolve these dilemmas for me.

Another possibility that I have considered is whether to position myself as a spiritual director (i.e. someone who people consult about their spiritual life). This has a strong attraction for me and I have had some limited training and experience of this way of working and being. However, in itself it does not appear to resolve the dilemmas for me, more to sidestep it by moving into a more comfortable position.

It feels as if I need to continue to therapeutically engage with people (clients) in a spiritual context and in a sufficiently open and creative way to allow me to be as useful as possible for them. Currently the best fitting label for me remains 'counsellor'. Any new label would raise questions relating to professional practice, ethics, supervision and so on. However, I have a deep conviction that the progress of my current and future clients and my own growth and development are asking me to extend the ways in which I work therapeutically. If I were to choose a phrase that encapsulates the way I currently see myself working, it would be *soul attender* which according to Tick (1992) is a literal translation of the word psychotherapist when one returns to the original Greek. The notion of attending fits comfortably with my current experience of acting as a witness or midwife to my clients' unfolding spiritual process and it captures the idea of being with them rather than doing something to them. The use of the word 'soul' celebrates the spiritual that also includes how it is to be found in the depth of our being.

These speculations of mine find an echo in Brian Thorne's latest book (2002) in which he talks of the 'spiritual potency' of the person-centred therapist who can, according to Thorne, have the capacity of being both a secular priest and prophet. Thorne is laying claim to the innate spirituality to be found within the therapeutic encounter as practised by person-centred therapists. Again the person-centred world is another possible place for me to be. However, whilst deeply valuing the core conditions of congruence, empathy and positive unconditional regard that underpin their work, I am unable to accept that such conditions offered to and perceived by the clients involved are necessary and sufficient. Even Rogers (1980) speculated about adding his concept of presence to these conditions. I cannot make the act of faith involved. And of course the person-centred world is deeply split around spirituality and around which part of Rogers' life is the model to follow Chicago or California. Maybe the creative tension around all these matters makes me a better therapist, certainly a different one! I suspect it may never resolve.

Spiritual self care

It is not possible to be psychospiritually present within the spirit of this book without great self care. Montgomery's (1991) research with seasoned nurses points us to how burnout is best prevented by an active spiritual life. Rowan (1993) controversially

advocated that all therapists address their needs to develop spirituality. I still hold back from such a position but I do maintain that
unless therapists do that then they will be less effective for their
clients around issues to do with spirituality. Indeed I would argue
that to work at a spiritual depth with a client requires the therapist to practise their own spiritual discipline. None of this can or
should be forced, it has its own time, place and space which in
itself needs honouring. Developing ourselves spiritually should
not feel like an abusive process, painful at times as we face difficult
truths about ourselves and creation but not abusive. For me it
seems natural that those of us awake to our spirituality would pursue
a path of spiritual development. Such a process could involve:

- regular meditation (as with Geller's (2001) therapists who
  use presence);
- contemplation;
- prayer;
- Tai Chi or Yoga;
- Time in the countryside;
- Spiritual journal writing;
- Spiritual friendships and direction;
- Retreats; and
- Anything else that helps one develop spiritually.

The aim of this being to keep the practitioner spiritually fit enough
to be psychospritually present to her or his clients.

Brian Thorne (2002) has put forward his recommendations for
his secular priests/person-centred therapists. This includes: beginning with self-love; compassion towards our own body; holding
our clients in mind on a regular basis; having a connection to
nature and human creativity; and waiting upon the invisible
world. He suggests that we seek a spiritual discipline that fits us:
'To put it as succinctly as possible, the person-centred therapist
who commits himself or herself to the living out of the core conditions is exercising the spiritual discipline which is the expression of
a practical mysticism' (Thorne 2002 p. 84).

Sin, forgiveness, repentance and revenge

It might seem strange to discuss the matter of sin in a book about
counselling and psychotherapy but hopefully not so inappropriate

in a book on spirituality and matters of the human soul. According to a Jewish friend of mine the notion of sin in that tradition is best understood or translated as having missed the mark which usually gets us away from merely beating our chests and sinking into masochists slough and it invites us to focus on how to improve our aims.

Indeed it seems to me under the influence of the 14th-century mystic Julian of Norwich (Grace Jantzen's (1987) book on Julian is a treat) that sin is unavoidable, that God wishes us to engage with the world and inevitably sin which we then have to work through and if we complete this process we are better people than if we had never engaged with the world at all. As Grace quotes from Julian:

> By Contrition we are made clean, by compassion we are made ready, and by true longing for God we are made worthy. These are three means, as I understand, through which all souls come to heaven, those, that is to say, who have been sinners on earth and will be saved. For every sinful soul must be healed by these medicines. Though he be healed, his wounds are not seen by God as wounds but as honours...For he regards sin as sorrow and pains for his lovers to whom he assigns no blame.
>
> (Jantzen 1987 p. 2000)

In this sense I have sins around that which I did, which I bitterly regret and that which I did not do which I can be equally regretful of. But there is another source of sin and a need for forgiveness. I grew up with a relatively low sense of self-esteem and time and time again have turned away from achieving things because of such low self-regard. Indeed every new achievement in my life, including writing this, involves me battling yet again with this low self-regard. So I have to forgive myself for how this low self-esteem has prevented me from doing all that I knew I could do. This is really hard.

I know, think and feel that low self-esteem for me and others has to be addressed time and time again and that there is no quick or even slow therapeutic cure for it or at least not for me so far. I am not sure but I guess low self-esteem is part of our Christian culture at least among the Anglo Saxon English – 'Don't get above yourself', 'pride goes before a fall', 'you are so sharp you will cut yourself'.

This goes even deeper for me because all the new developments in my life have involved me moving on psychologically and/or physically. Each new step involves a letting go of people and places and an openness to the new and a trust that the new will manifest, it does not get easier, if anything harder though these days I do trust more. This can feel lonely and I do recognise that I was afraid of the loneliness of moving on following my spiritual path. Then I was helped to see that actually it is the loneliness that I have in my everyday life that is the problem not the loneliness of moving on, and then I was further helped to explore the difference between being alone and being lonely.

I was enabled at one time in a sacro-cranial session to be given a kind of vision of a time soon after my birth when things change from everything being OK to some split-off state that left a deep split inside of me and an inevitable feeling of not being OK and not being treated OK in some basic way from then on. My spiritual faith and practice enables me to live with this existential terror and provides me with fleeting spiritual experiences of being whole, which although impossible to hang on to leave their traces nonetheless.

Brian Thorne (1988) writes interestingly about original sin and points us to the idea of original righteousness suggesting that low self-worth could be seen as the origins of sin and implying that our lack of contact with our spirituality, with something bigger than ourselves, with God if you like causes us to feel bad about ourselves which in some way does connect with what I have just written in the above paragraph.

One of the dangers of a too simplistic understanding of a psychodynamic position is to view our problems as stemming from imperfect parents and that if only we could successfully heal our childhood wounds then we could become the people we were intended to be. Wilhelm Reich (1952) spoke movingly of how you cannot straighten a bent tree, but a tree growing around a stone has its own beauty in my eyes. True therapy should help us love our actual shape, not dream of what could be despite our knowing in our bones it could and should be different. What is the best we can do now? At this point I will repeat the words of the Catholic writer Henri Nouwen (1989): 'Forgiveness is the name of love practiced among people who love poorly. The hard truth is that all of us love poorly. We need to forgive and be forgiven every day, every hour-unceasingly. That is the great work of love among the fellowship of the weak that is the human family.'

Appropriate supervision

I am still puzzled by how many seemingly experienced therapists end up in supervision relationships that are not very helpful at the very least. Such relationships need to be ended and hopefully in a no blame 'divorce'. We deserve better. Effective supervision demands a maturity on both sides so that the supervision is alive and developing at not merely something one sits out once a month for an hour or so! I have found great value in having more than one supervisor when the tasks are made clear. Other people I know also use group supervision in addition to individual supervision. Having differing views on the same experience can be most helpful.

In terms of supervision of psychospiritual work this will be impossible and possibly destructive if the supervisor is not respectful of religion and spirituality or welcoming of the broad sweep of the supervisee work in that domain. Issues around supervision, spirituality and therapy were explored fully in Chapter 5, all I wish to emphasise here is that careful contracting at the start of the supervision relationship is vital and such contracts should be renewed on a regular basis.

Courageous heart and soul

Following what may seem like a very intuitive thread into the psychospiritual realm with any one client takes great courage, great heart and great soul. It also takes a grounding as Geller's (2001) work showed and which was illustrated in my extended case study earlier. It does seem as if sometimes the most useful developments in the work with a particular client come out the seemingly absurd – passing images and words, fleeting bodily sensations and so on. Ignore these at your clients and your own peril. If a good therapeutic alliance has been established with a client and something is offered very tentatively (e.g. I might say, 'I suddenly have this most curious image or feeling...' and I wait to see if the client picks it up or not. Even if they do not it does not mean it was not accurate, possibly they were unable to use it at that moment in time) then the client can ignore it without any trouble or damage. However, not saying such things could very well leave a client unhelped or helped more slowly. I am quite content to leave a vague boundary between advanced empathy, intuition and something more explicitly spiritual.

Always acting ethically

It should be abundantly clear that working in a psychospiritual way requires careful attention to ethics. The new British Association for Counselling and Psychotherapy's Ethical Framework for Good Practice in Counselling and Psychotherapy (2001) has a focus on ethical principles underlying practice as a positive stance rather than unduly focusing on not doing this and not doing that. In the spirit I believe of this framework is Bond's (2000) advocacy of 'ethical mindfulness'. Such an approach invites us to do the work of engaging with our therapeutic behaviour ethically rather than relying on a code to tell us what to do. Psychospiritual work can be extraordinarily powerful and the therapist can all too readily be seen as some kind of spiritual teacher, guru or more developed being. Within the therapy room itself the boundary between client and therapist may seem somewhat blurred if something akin to the I–Thou type encounter happens. At such a moment the client may well feel very wide open and tender. Great care is needed.

Necessary knowledge

One of the joys of engaging in heuristic research processes is a clear recognition that we know more than we usually know we know. This is tacit knowledge, it is a kind of knowledge that comes to us spontaneously while meditating, walking or simply being with a client. A lot of our clinical practice unexamined occurs at this tacit level. One of the joys of supervision or writing about therapy is to make such tacit knowing more explicit. We have such tacit knowing about the culture and sub-culture we belong to. We naturally locate people regionally and in terms of their class, according to how they speak and we react as a result, often without thought. As trained therapists it is to be hoped that our clinical experience of the individual in front of us will modify any possible prejudices we might thus have formed about them.

There is an argument advanced in person-centred circles (discussed critically in Laungani 1997, 2001) that as therapists we do not need to study culture merely to listen to what our client is telling us about his or her culture. It is a seemingly attractive notion but I believe it will not do. Whilst it is true that we need to hear how our client is experiencing their culture, it is ignorant of us not to have some broad takes on key aspects of the many cultures that we are likely to come across. Two examples might suffice, I was recently in conversation with a 2nd generation South Asian woman about someone I knew who was going to do research into arranged marriages. She asked me to clarify whether I meant, 'forced' or 'arranged' marriages, an important distinction that differentiates between what might seem a curious but traditional way of arranging a marriage and the use of intimidation to bring about a marriage. A second example of that of an Islamic female Sudanese woman who I taught some years ago. She did not make eye contact with me nor with other tutors and she never volunteered a contribution to discussions or seminars. She later explained to me in a tutorial that a good Muslim woman in her culture did not make eye contact nor offer opinions unasked. From then on when I invited her contributions to seminars she was very forthcoming and insightful.

The more I engage with other cultures especially around religion and spirituality, the more I am led to explore and understand more deeply my own roots, things that I hitherto might just have taken for granted or accepted on a tacit level. Sometimes this has led me into exploring much of what was seemingly forgotten in the mainstream part of my culture. My assumption is that all cultures in some ways deal with the same basic spiritual questions of who we are, what are we here for and so on. From a deeper understanding of my own culture I can then move out and contact with other cultures, relate to what I find, when I can, and above all, allow myself to be changed in the process. When I accept and give value to the spirituality of another person whose spirituality is different to mine it changes my relationship with my own spirituality. It is a great cure for spiritual and religious one-upmanship and I think it is part of the spirit within which Ken Wilber has done his great work. I see much to admire in Buddhism, Sikhism, Judaism, Islam, Paganism and many New Age forms of spirituality. I have a problem with fundamentalists who will not respect my own spiritual journeying, nevertheless I have had tender meetings with a number of them.

I burn with a desire to learn and experience more of these things and it is this passion that I bring to my psychospiritual work with clients, albeit tempered and tamed by their particular therapeutic needs of that time. What it does mean is that I no longer wish to work therapeutically with people who do not accept, or who maybe even deny, their spiritual nature. There are plenty of secular therapists to choose from in the large multicultural city I belong to.

An agenda for change

So how might we bring about this psychospiritual practitioner? Clearly there are many therapists already working at least some of the time in the spirit of the psychospiritual discussed in this book. To bring about an effective and developed counselling and psychotherapy profession committed to their clients' psychospiritual developmental needs, the following agenda should prove helpful:

1   An inclusion of a substantial training around spiritual issues in basic counselling and psychotherapist training courses with BACP, UKCP support for this measure. This reflects the needs and views of many trainees (Swinton 1996).
2   Specialised working with spirituality post training courses for therapists already trained or who want to update and upgrade their skills.
3   The contents of such a training package could include all or some of the following: religion, spirituality and culture in Britain today; Wilber and other psychospiritual maps; spiritual experience; diagnostic issues; counter transference; pastoral care and referrals; spiritual interventions in therapy.
4   Further development of theories, maps and sense-making around spirituality and therapy.
5   Further research into religiosity of therapists and their attitude to spirituality; therapists' use of spiritual interventions (quantitative and qualitative); outcomes of spiritual interventions.
6   Personal development work around therapist's own spirituality.
7   Considering spirituality in a postmodern or post postmodern context.

Future possibilities

Active engagement with the above agenda would totally change how the world of therapy relates to the universe of the client's (and the therapist's) spirituality. Given the rough equality of outcomes between the differing schools of therapy addressing differing issues (Shapiro *et al.* 2000) the key outcome research question now, I believe, focuses on the individual therapist and their fit with their client. Introducing the question of spirituality into the therapist/client relationship does add an extra variable but does also permit the possibility of a greater fit between both therapist and client or rather can add to the choice that could be made available to the client. Gordon Lynch's (2002) discussion of the 'good life' and our views of it as practitioner is helpful here. There has, I believe, to be some shared values between therapist and client and one key feature of this is certainly attitude, explicitly or implicitly, to spirituality. Extending therapist competence and extending client choice can only benefit the client in the long run.

It is perfect

Just as I was putting the finishing touches to this book my father died rather suddenly of a heart attack at the age of 90. In the days following his death and subsequent funeral, I passed through a whole gamut of feelings or rather they passed through me – anger, grief, emptiness, pointlessness, shock, dread, you name it I felt it. Then it occurred to me that what I was feeling was perfect. There was no better, no more spiritual state to be in. So I briefly felt better about these difficult feelings I was having, briefly more willing to honour them as part of life and death.

Conclusion

I am not naïve enough to believe that the therapy world as a whole will enthusiastically embrace my view of the importance of therapists honouring their clients' (and their own) spirituality. Nevertheless I do feel that a careful consideration of spirituality in its healthy and less healthy forms should now be seen as an essential and necessary part of effective therapy. After all why practise with one arm behind your back? If spirituality is healthy and important to your client why not use it to help their growth?

However, religion has aided and abetted some of the worse horrors of human existence including its recent role in the horrendous attack on the USA on September 11 and the subsequent bombing of Afghanistan. As I write now, the war on Iraq is more or less over though it still has unpredictable consequences. It would be easy, but too easy, to suggest that we have nothing to do with religion and spirituality in the light of such madness. Nevertheless on the other side of this coin is another truth of how religions and spirituality have inspired people to great acts of compassion and social change. The role of such people in the development in Britain of counselling, psychotherapy, and other helping professions such as social work, occupational therapy and so on is under-recognised.

Spiritual experiences mostly change people for the better. Without the sense of our interconnectedness, a move away from materialism, and a developing sense of the sacredness of life and the whole of creation, which are a common feature of such experiences it would seem to me that our very future as a species will not just be in the balance but will tip over into destruction. Therapy which if it seeks to promote true health by engaging with the depth of human experience must engage with the wider society and with our spirituality. This is the real place for soul attending, nothing less will do.

Bibliography

Akbar, N. (1984) *The Community of Self* (Tallahassee, FL: Mind Productions).

Akbar, N. (1994) *Light from Ancient Africa* (Tallahassee, FL: Mind Productions).

Alexander, F. (1931) 'Buddhist training as artificial catatonia', *Psychoanalytic Review*, 18: 129–145.

Allman, L. S., De La Rocha, O., Elkins, D. N. and Weathers, R. S. (1992) 'Psychotherapists' attitudes towards clients reporting mystical experiences', *Psychotherapy*, 29(4): 654–569.

Allport, G. W. and Ross, J. M. (1967) 'Personal religious orientation and prejudice', *Journal of Personality and Social Psychology*, 5: 432–443.

American Psychological Association (1994) *Diagnostic and Statistical Manual of Mental Disorders IV* (Washington, DC: APA).

Angus, L. E. and Rennie, D. L. (1988) 'Therapists participation in metaphor generation: collaborative and noncollaborative styles', *Psychotherapy*, 25: 552–560.

Ankrah, L. (2000) 'Experiences of dealing with spiritual emergency within counselling relationships', unpublished MA thesis, University of Manchester.

Ankrah, L. (2002) 'Spiritual emergency and counselling: an exploratory study', *Counselling and Psychotherapy Research*, 2(1): 55–60.

Anthony, R., Ecker, B. and Wilber, K. (eds) (1987) *Spiritual Choices* (New York: Paragon House).

Arbuckle, D. S. (1968) 'Counselling effectiveness and related issues', *Journal of Counselling Psychology*, 15(5): 430–435.

Assagioli, R. (1986) 'Self-realisation and psychological disturbance', *Revision*, 8(2): 21–31.

Backhouse, H. (ed.) (1988) *The Dark Night of the Soul, St John of the Cross* (London: Hodder and Stoughton).

Baldwin, M. (ed.) (2000) *The Use of Self in Therapy*, 2nd edition (New York: Haworth).

Barker, E. (1989) *New Religious Movements, An Introduction* (London: HMSO).

Barks, C. (1995) *The Essential Rumi* (London: Penguin).

Bates, B. (1993) 'Visions of reality in shamanic psychology', *Changes*, 11(3): 223–228.

Benner, D. G. (1988) *Psychotherapy and the Spiritual Quest* (Michigan, USA: Baker Book House).

Bergen, A. E. (1980) 'Psychotherapy and religious values', *Journal of Consulting and Clinical Psychology*, 48: 75–105.

Bergen, A. E. and Jensen, J. P. (1990) 'Religiosity of psychotherapists: a national survey', *Psychotherapy*, **27**: 3–7.

Bilgrave, D. P. and Deluty, R. H. (1998) 'Religious beliefs and therapeutic orientations of clinical and counseling psychologists', *Journal for the Scientific Study of Religion*, **37**(2): 329–349.

Boadella, D. (1973) *Wilhelm Reich, the Evolution of his Work* (Chicago: Contemporary Books).

Bolger, E. A. (1999) 'Grounded theory analysis of emotional pain, *Psychotherapy Research*, **9**(3): 342–362.

Bond, M. S. (2002) 'Counselling and ministry: a reflexive hermeneutic study', MA thesis, University of Abertay, Dundee.

Bond, T. (2000) *Standards and Ethics for Counselling in Action*, 2nd edition (London: Sage).

Boorstein, S. (ed.) (1986) *Transpersonal Psychotherapy* (Palo Alto, CA: Science & Behavior Books).

Boucouvalas, M. (1980) 'Transpersonal psychology: an outline of the field', *Journal of Transpersonal Psychology*, **12**(10): 37–46.

Brazier, D. (1996) 'A Zen response', *Self & Society*, **24**(4): 15–18.

Brierley, P. (1991) *Prospects for the Nineties, all England Trends and Tables from the English Church Census, with Denominations and Churchmanships* (London: MARC Europe).

Brierley, P. (2000) *Religious Trends, No. 2: 1999/2000* (London: Christian Research).

British Association for Counselling and Psychotherapy (2001) *Ethical Framework for Good Practice in Counselling and Psychotherapy* (Rugby: BACP).

Bruce, S. (1995a) *Religion in Modern Britain* (Oxford: Oxford University Press).

Bruce, S. (1995b) 'The truth about religion in Britain', *Journal for the Scientific Study of Religion*, **34**(4): 417–430.

Buber, M. (1923/1970) *I and Thou* (Edinburgh: T & T Clark).

Byrd, R. C. (1988) 'Positive therapeutic effects of intercessory prayer in coronary care unit population', *Southern Medical Journal*, **81**: 826–929.

Carlat, D. J. (1989) 'Psychological motivation and the choice of spiritual symbols: a case study', *Journal of Transpersonal Psychology*, **21**(2): 139–148.

Chaplin, J. (1989) 'Rhythm and blues', in W. Dryden and L. Spurling (eds), *On Becoming a Psychotherapist* (London: Tavistock/Routledge).

Charmaz, K. (2000) 'Grounded theory: objectionist and constructionist methods', in N. K. Denzin and Y. S. Lincoln (eds), *Handbook of Qualitative Research*, 2nd edition (London: Sage).

Clark, F. V. (1979) 'Exploring intuition: prospects and possibilities', *Journal of Transpersonal Psychology*, **5**(2): 156–170.

Clarkson, P. (1990) 'A multiplicity of therapeutic relationships', *British Journal of Psychotherapy*, **7**(2): 148–163.

Claxton, G. (1996) 'Therapy and beyond: concluding thoughts', in G. Claxton (ed.), *Beyond Therapy: The Impact of Eastern Religions on Psychological Theory and Practice* (Dorset: Prism).

Clinton, J. (2002) 'Not enough love', *The Friend*, 23 August, p. 13.

Cooper, D. (1970) *Psychiatry and Anti Psychiatry* (London: Paladin).

Cushman, P. (1990) 'Why the self is empty, towards a historically situated psychology', *American Psychologist*, May, pp. 599–611.

Cushman, P. (1995) *Constructing the Self, Constructing America, a Cultural History of Psychotherapy* (New York: Perseus).

Dandelion, B. P. (1996) *A Sociological Analysis of the Theology of Quakers* (Lampeter: Edmin Mellen).

Davie, G. (1994) *Religion in Britain since 1945* (Oxford: Blackwell).

Davy, L. (2001) 'A study of counsellors' attitudes towards spirituality and well being, and spiritual awareness in counsellor training', MA Dissertation, Faculty of Education, University of Manchester.

Deikman, A. J. (1982) *The Observing Self: Mysticism and Psychotherapy* (Boston: Beacon).

Denzin, N. K. (1989) *Interpretive Interactionism* (Newbury Park, CA: Sage).

Denzin, N. K. and Lincoln, Y. S. (eds) (1994) *Handbook of Qualitative Research* (California: Sage).

Denzin, N. K. and Lincoln, Y. S. (eds) (2000) *Handbook of Qualitative Research*, 2nd edition (California: Sage).

DiBlasio, F. A. and Proctor, J. H. (1993) 'Therapists and the clinical use of forgiveness', *American Journal of Family Therapy*, 21(2): 175–183.

Dorff, E. N. (1998) 'The elements of forgiveness: a Jewish approach', in E. L. Worthington (ed.), *Dimensions of Forgiveness: Psychological Research and Theological Perspectives* (London: Templeton Foundation).

Douglass, B. G. and Moustakas, C. (1985) 'Heuristic inquiry: the internal search to know', *Journal of Humanistic Psychology*, 25(3): 39–55.

Edwards, G. (1992) 'Does psychotherapy need a soul?', in W. Dryden and C. Feltham (eds), *Psychotherapy and its Discontents* (Buckingham: Open University Press).

Einstein, A. (1954) *Ideas and Opinions* (New York: The Modern Library).

Eliade, M. (1960) *Myths, Dreams and Mysteries* (New York: Harper & Row).

Eliade, M. (1964) *Shamanism, Archaic Techniques of Ecstasy* (Princeton, NJ: Princeton University Press).

Elkins, D. N., Hedstorm, L. J., Hughes, L. L., Leaf, J. A. and Saunders, C. (1988) 'Towards a humanistic-phenomenological spirituality', *Journal of Humanistic Psychology*, 28(4): 5–18.

Ellenberger, H. (1970) *The Discovery of the Unconscious* (New York: Basic Books).

Enright, D. (1996) 'Counseling within the forgiveness triad: on forgiving, receiving forgiveness, and self-forgiving', *Counsel and Values*, 40(2): 107–126.

Enright, R. D. and Coyle, C. T. (1998) 'Researching the process model of forgiveness with psychological interventions', in E. L. Worthington (ed.), *Dimensions of Forgiveness: Psychological Research and Theological Perspectives* (London: Templeton Foundation).

Erikson, E. (1977) *Childhood and Society* (London: Paladin).

Farrow, J. (1984) 'Spirituality and self-awareness', *Friends Quarterly*, July, pp. 213–323.

Feltham, C. (1995) *What is Counselling?* (London: Sage).

Feltham, C. (2002) 'A surveillance culture?', *Counselling and Psychotherapy Journal*, **13**(1): 26–27.

Ferguson, D. S. (ed.) (1993) *New Age Spirituality* (Louisville, Kentucky: Westminster/John Knox Press).

Fielding, R. G. and Llewelyn, S. (1996) 'The new religions and psychotherapy: similarities and differences', in G. Claxton (ed.), *Beyond Therapy: The Impact of Eastern Religions on Psychological Theory and Practice* (Dorset: Prism).

Forst, E. and Healy, R. M. (1990) 'Relationship between self-esteem and religious faith', *Psychological Reports*, **67**: 378.

Foskett, J. and Jacobs, M. (1989) 'Pastoral counselling', in W. Dryden, D. Charles-Richards and R. Woolfe (eds), *Handbook of Counselling in Britain* (London: Tavistock/Routledge).

Foskett, J. and Lyall, D. (1988) *Helping the Helpers* (London: SPCK).

Fowler, J. W. (1981) *Stages of Faith: The Psychology of Human Development and the Quest for Meaning* (New York: Harper & Row).

Fox, M. (1993) 'Spirituality for a new era', in D. S. Ferguson (ed.), *New Age Spirituality* (Louisville, Kentucky: Westminster/John Knox Press).

Frankl, V. E. (1947) *The Unconscious God* (New York: Simon & Schuster).

Frankl, V. E. (1973) *The Doctor and the Soul, from Psychotherapy to Logotherapy* (London: Pelican).

Frankl, V. E. (1978) *Man's Search for Meaning* (London: Hodder & Stoughton).

Freud, S. (1933) *New Introductory Lectures of Psychoanalysis* (London: Hogarth Press).

Freud, S. (1963) *Civilization and its Discontents* (New York: Basic Books).

Friedman, M. (1993) *Religion and Psychotherapy: A Dialogical Approach* (New York: Paragon House).

Fromm, E. (1950) *Psychoanalysis and Religion* (New Haven, NJ: Yale University Press).

Fromm, E. (1986) *Psychoanalysis and Zen Buddhism* (London: Unwin).

Fuller, R. C. (1984) 'Rogers's impact on pastoral counseling and contemporary religious reflection', in R. F. Levant and J. M. Shlien (eds), *Client-Centered Therapy and the Person-Centered Approach* (New York: Praeger).

Geller, S. (2001) 'Therapists' presence: the development of a model and a measure', Doctoral dissertation, York University, Toronto, Canada.

Geller, S. M. and Greenberg, L. S. (2002) 'Therapeutic presence: therapists' experience of presence in the psychotherapy encounter', *Person-Centred and Experiential Therapies*, 1: 71–86.

Gendlin, E. (1978) *Focusing* (New York: Bantam Books).

Gergen, K. J. (1985) 'The social constuctionist movement in modern psychology', *American Psychologist*, 40: 266–275.

Gergen, K. J. (1988) 'If persons are texts', in S. B. Messer, L. A. Sass and R. L. Woolfolk (eds), *Hermeneutics and Psychological Theory: Interpretive Perspectives on Personality, Psychotherapy and Psychopathology* (New Brunswick, NJ: Rutgers University Press).

Gergen, K. J. (1991) *The Saturated Self: Dilemmas of Identity in Modern Life* (New York: Basic Books).

Gergen, K. J. (1996) 'Post modern society as a concept, introductory lecture at International Conference for Psychotherapy', Vienna, July, audio tape.

Gillman, H. (1988) *A Light that is Shining* (London: Quaker Home Service).

Glaser, B. (1992) *Emergence v Forcing: Basics of Grounded Theory Analysis* (California: Sociology Press).

Glaser, B. and Strauss, A. (1967) *The Discovery of Grounded Theory* (Chicago: Aldine).

Goodman, F. D. (1986) 'Body posture and the religious altered state of consciousness: an experiential investigation', *Journal of Humanistic Psychology*, 26(3): 81–118.

Grof, S. (1972) 'Varieties of transpersonal experiences: observations from LSD psychotherapy', *Journal of Transpersonal Psychology*, 4(1): 45–80.

Grof, C. and Grof, S. (1986) 'Spiritual emergency: the understanding and treatment of transpersonal crisis', *Revision*, 8(2): 7–20.

Grof, S. and Grof, C. (1989) *Spiritual Emergency* (Los Angeles: Tarcher).

Gubi, P. (2000) 'Prayer and psychotherapy – an exploration of the therapeutic nature of Christian prayer and its possible use with Christian clients in secular psychotherapy', paper to 6th Annual BACP Counselling Research Conference, Manchester, 20 May.

Gubi, P. (2001) 'An exploration of the use of Christian prayer in mainstream Counselling', *British Journal of Guidance and Counselling*, 29(5): 425–434.

Gubi, P. (2002) 'Practice behind closed doors: challenging the taboo of prayer in mainstream counselling culture', *Journal of Critical Psychology, Counselling and Psychotherapy*, 2(2): 97–104.

Gubi, P. (2003) 'Integrating prayer and counselling: an enquiry into mainstream counsellors whose work includes prayer', PhD thesis, Faculty of Education, University of Manchester.

Guenther, M. (1992) *Holy Listening: The Art of Spiritual Direction* (London: Darton, Longman and Todd).

Guest, H. (1989) 'The origins of transpersonal psychology', *British Journal of Psychology*, 6(1): 62–69.

Guntrip, H. (1956) *Mental Pain and the Cure of Souls* (London: Independent Press).

Hall, J. (1990) 'Transformation in counselling', *British Journal of Guidance and Counselling*, **18**(3): 269–280.

Halmos, P. (1965) *The Faith of the Counsellors* (London: Constable).

Hardy, A. (1979) *The Spiritual Nature of Man* (Oxford: Clarendon Press).

Hawkins, P. and Shohet, R. (1989) *Supervision in the Helping Professions* (Milton Keynes: Open University Press).

Hay, D. (1982) *Exploring Inner Space: Scientists and Religious Experience* (Harmondsworth, Middlesex: Penguin).

Hay, D. (1979) 'Religious experience among a group of post graduate students – a qualitative study', *Journal for the Scientific Study of Religion*, **18**(2): 164–182.

Hay, D. and Hunt, K. (2000) *Understanding the Spirituality of People Who Don't go to Church* (Centre for the Study of Human relations, Nottingham University).

Hay, D. and Morisy, A. (1978) 'Reports of ecstatic, paranormal, or religious experiences in Great Britain and the United States – a comparison of trends', *Journal for the Scientific Study of Religion*, **17**(3): 255–268.

Healey, B. J. (1993) 'Psychotherapy and religious experience: integrating psychoanalytic psychotherapy with Christian religious experience', in G. Stricker and J. R. Gold (eds), *Comprehensive Handbook of Psychotherapy Integration* (New York: Plenum Press).

Heelas, P. and Kohn, R. (1996) 'Psychotherapy and techniques of transformation', in G. Claxton (ed.), *Beyond Therapy: The Impact of Eastern Religions on Psychological Theory and Practice* (Dorset: Prism).

Heron, J. (1992) *Feeling and Personhood* (London: Sage).

Heron, J. (1998) *Sacred Science, Person-Centred Inquiry into the Spiritual and Subtle* (Ross-on-Wye: PCCS Books).

Hollanders, H. (1997) 'Eclecticism/Integration among Counsellors in the Light of Kuhn's Concept of Paradigm Formation', Doctoral thesis, Department of Applied Social Studies, Keele University.

Hollanders, H. (2000) 'Eclecticism/integration: Some key issues and research', in S. Palmer and R. Woolfe (eds), *Integrative and Eclectic Counselling and Psychotherapy*, pp. 31–55 (London: Sage).

Hollanders, H. and McLeod, J. (1997) 'Theoretical orientation and reported practice: a survey of eclecticism among counsellors in Britain', *British Journal of Guidance and Counselling*, **27**(3): 405–414.

Horney, K. (1942) *Self-Analysis* (New York: Norton).

Hopson, R. E. (1996) 'The 12-step program', in E. P. Shafranske (ed.), *Religion and the Clinical Practice of Psychology*, pp. 533–558 (Washington, DC: American Psychological Association).

Howard, A. (1995) *Challenging Counselling and Psychotherapy* (London: Macmillan).

Howard, A. (2000) *Philosophy for Counselling and Psychotherapy* (London: Macmillan).

Hughes, G. W. (1985) *God of Surprises* (London: Darton, Longman and Todd).

Isbister, J. N. (1985) *Freud, an Introduction to his Life and Work* (Cambridge: Polity Press).

Jacobs, M. (1991) 'The therapist's revenge: the law of talion as a motive for caring', *Contact*, 2: 2–11.

Jackson, M. L. (1995) 'Multicultural counseling, historic perspectives', in J. G. Ponterotto, J. M. Cases, L. A. Suzuki and C. M. Alexander (eds), *Handbook of Multi Cultural Counseling* (Thousand Oaks, CA: Sage).

James, W. (1901) *The Varieties of Religious Experience* (London: Collins).

Jantzen, G. (1987) *Julian of Norwich* (London: SPCK).

Jantzen, G. (2002) 'For an engaged reading: William James and the varieties of postmodern religious experience', paper to Conference on William James, Edinburgh, June.

Jeff, M. (1987) *Spiritual Direction for Every Christian* (London: SPCK).

Jenkins, C. (2003) 'Third time lucky? Issues in counselling and spirituality raised by a research interview and a personal encounter', unpublished paper.

Jones, D. (1994) *Innovative Therapies: A Handbook* (Buckingham: Open University Press).

Jones, D. (1996) 'The psychospiritual: psychospiritual and transpersonal psychotherapies', *Self & Society*, 24(4): 4–6.

Jones, E. (1953) *Sigmund Freud, Life and work, Vol 1* (London: Hogarth).

Jones, R. (1921) *The Later Periods of Quakerism* (London: Macmillan).

Jung, C. G. (1933) *Modern Man in Search of a Soul* (London: Routledge and Kegan Paul).

Jung, C. G. (1958) *Psychology and Religion* (London: Routledge & Kegan Paul).

Jung, C. G. (1967) *Memories, Dreams, Reflections* (London: Fontana).

Jung, C. G. (1968) *Aion: Researches in the Phenomenology of the Self* (London: Routledge).

Kaberry, S. (2000) 'Abuse in supervision', in B. Lawton and C. Feltham (eds), *Taking Supervision Forward: Dilemmas, Insights and Trends* (London: Sage).

Kirschenbaum, H. and Henderson, V. (eds) (1990a) *The Carl Rogers Reader* (London: Constable).

Kirschenbaum, H. and Henderson, V. (eds) (1990b) *Carl Rogers Dialogues* (London: Constable).

Kirschner, S. R. (1996) *The Religious and Romantic Origins of Psychoanalysis* (Cambridge: Cambridge University Press).

Knott, K. (1988) 'Other major religious traditions', in T. Thomas (ed.), *The British: Their Religious Beliefs and Practices 1800–1986* (London: Routledge).

Krippner, S. (1992) 'The shamen as healer and psychotherapist', *Voices, the Art and Science of Psychotherapy*, Winter, pp. 12–23.

Krishnamurti, J. (1975) *Life Ahead* (NewYork: Harper & Row).

Kvale, S. (1992) 'Postmodern psychology: a contradiction in terms?', in S. Kvale (ed.), *Psychology and Postmodernism* (London: Sage).

Kubler-Ross, E. (1997) *The Wheel of Life* (London: Bantam).

Ladany, N., Lehrman-Waterman, D. E., Molinaro, M. and Wolgast, B. (1999) 'Psychotherapy supervisor ethical practices: adherence to guidelines, the supervisory working alliance and supervisee satisfaction', *Counseling Psychologist*, 27: 443–475.

Ladany, N. and Muse-Burke, J. L. (2001) 'Understanding and conducting supervision research', in L. J. Bradley and N. Ladany (eds), *Counselor Supervision: Principles, Process and Practice* (Pennsylvania: Brunner-Routledge).

Lago, C. and Thompson, J. (1996) *Race, Culture and Counselling* (Buckingham: Open University Press).

Laing, R. D. (1967) *The Politics of Experience* (New York: Ballantine).

Laing, R. D. (1972) 'Metanoia: some experiences at Kingsley Hall, London', in H. M. Ruitenbeck (ed.), *Going Crazy* (New York: Bantam).

Laing, R. D. (1985) *Wisdom, Madness and Folly, The Making of a Psychiatrist, 1927–1957* (London: Macmillan).

Lake, F. (1981) *Tight Corners in Pastoral Counselling* (London: Darton, Longman and Todd).

Lannert, J. L. (1991) 'Resistance and countertransference issues with spiritual and religious clients', *Journal of Humanistic Psychology*, 31(4): 68–76.

Larty, E. (1997) *In Living Colour* (London: Cassell).

Laungani, P. (1997) 'Replacing client-centred counselling with culture-centred counselling', *Counselling Psychology Quarterly*, 10(4): 343–351.

Laungani, P. (2001) 'Cross-cultural psychology: a handmaiden to mainstream Western psychology: a personal view', key note address to 1st International Conference of South Asia Regional Conference, Mumbai India, December.

Laungani, P. (2003) *Asian Perspectives in Counselling and Psychotherapy* (London: Routledge) (at press).

Lee, C. C. and Armstrong, K. L. (1995) 'Indigenous models of mental health interventions: lessons from traditional healers', in J. G. Ponterotto, J. M. Cases, L. A. Suzuki and C. M. Alexander (eds), *Handbook of Multi Cultural Counseling* (Thousand Oaks, CA: Sage).

Leech, K. (1994) *Soul Friend* (London: Darton, Longman and Todd).

Levine, S. (2000) *Who Dies: An Investigation of Conscious Living and Conscious Dying* (London: Gill and Macmillan).

Lèvi-Strauss, L. (1966) *The Savage Mind* (Chicago: University of Chicago Press).

Levy, J. (1983) 'Transpersonal and Jungian Psychology', *Journal of Humanistic Psychology*, 23(2): 42–51.

Lovinger, R. J. (1984) *Working with Religious Issues in Therapy* (New York: Jason Aronson).

Lukoff, D. (1985) 'The diagnosis of mystical experiences with psychotic features', *Journal of Transpersonal Psychology*, 17(2): 155–181.

Lukoff, D., Lu, F. and Turner, R. (1992) 'Toward a more culturally sensitive DSM IV', *Journal of Nervous and Mental Disease*, **180**(11): 673–682.

Lyall, D. (1995) *Counselling in the Pastoral and Spiritual Context* (Buckingham: Open University Press).

Lynch, G. (2000) 'Pastoral counselling in the new millennium', *Counselling*, **11**(6): 340–342.

Lynch, G. (1999) 'Pastoral counselling in a postmodern world, in G. Lynch (ed.), *Clinical Counselling in Pastoral Settings* (London: Routledge).

Lynch, G. (2002) *Pastoral Care and Counselling* (London: Sage).

Mackay, H., West, W., Moorey, J., Guthrie, E. and Margison, F. (2001) 'Counsellors' experiences of changing their practice: learning the psychodynamic-interpersonal model of therapy', *Counselling and Psychotherapy Research*, **1**(1), 29.

Mansor, A. T. (2002) 'Analysing transcripts about spirituality in counselling and psychotherapy: an outsider interpretation', unpublished paper.

Martin, J. and Thoresen, C. E. (1997) 'A cognitive-behavioral intervention model for forgiveness', unpublished manuscript, Stanford University.

Maslow, A. H. (1970) *Religions, Values, and Peak Experiences* (New York: Viking).

McCullough, M. E. and Worthington, E. L. (1994) 'Models of interpersonal forgiveness and their application to counseling: review and critique', *Counseling and Values*, **39**(1): 2–14.

McCullough, M. E., Pargament, K. I. and Thoresen, C. E. (eds) (2000) *Forgiveness: Theory, Research, and Practice* (New York: Guildford).

McCullough, M. E., Weaver, A. J., Larson, D. B. and Aay, K. R. (2000) 'Psychotherapy with mainline protestants: Lutheran, Presbyterian, Episcopal/ Anglican and Methodist', in P. S. Richards and A. E. Bergin (eds), *Handbook of Psychotherapy and Religious Diversity* (Washington, DC: American Psychological Association).

McLeod, J. (1990) 'The client's experience of counselling and psychotherapy: a review of the research literature', in D. Mearns and W. Dryden (eds), *Experiences of Counselling in Action* (London: Sage).

McLeod, J. (1993) *Introduction to Counselling* (Buckingham: Open University Press).

McLeod, J. (1997) *Narrative and Psychotherapy* (London: Sage).

McLeod, J. (1998) *Introduction to Counselling*, 2nd edition (Buckingham: Open University Press).

McLeod, J. (2001a) *Qualitative Research in Counselling and Psychotherapy* (London: Sage).

McLeod, J. (2001b) 'Counselling as a social process', in P. Milner and S. Palmer (eds), *The BACP Reader*, Vol. 2 (London: Sage).

McLeod, J. (2003) *Doing Counselling Research*, 2nd edition (London: Sage).

McLynn, F. (1996) *Carl Gustav Jung* (London: Black Swan).

McNeice, M. (1996) 'Premature forgiveness', *Self & Society*, **24**(2): 11–13.

McNeill, J. T. (1951) *A History of the Cure of Souls* (New York: Harper & Row).

Mearns, D. (1994) *Developing Person-Centred Counselling* (London: Sage).

Mearns, D. and Thorne, B. (1988) *Person-Centred Counselling in Action* (London: Sage).

Mellor-Clark, J., Connell, J., Barkham, M. and Cummins, P. (2001) 'Primary health care, a CORE systems profile', *European Journal of Psychotherapy, Counselling and Health*, **4**(1): 65–86.

Montgomery, C. E. (1991) 'The care-giving relationship: paradoxical and transcendent aspects', *Journal of Transpersonal Psychology*, **23**(2): 91–104.

Moodley, R. (1998) '"I say what I like": frank talk(ing) in counselling and Psychotherapy', *British Journal of Guidance and Counselling*, **26**(4): 495–508.

Moodley, R. (1999) 'Challenges and transformations: counselling in a multi-cultural context', *International Journal for the Advancement of Counselling*, **21**: 139–152.

Moore, T. (ed.) (1990) *The Essential James Hillman* (London: Routledge).

Moore, M. (2002) *Stupid White Men* (Harmondsworth: Penguin).

Morse, J. (1994) (ed.) *Critical Issues in Qualitative Research Methods* (London: Sage).

Moustakas, C. (1990) *Heuristic Research, Design, Methodology and Applications* (California: Sage).

Moustakas, C. (1994) *Phenomenological Research Methods* (London: Sage).

Nelson, S. H. and Torrey, E. F. (1973) 'The religious function of psychiatry', *American Journal of Orthopsychiatry*, **43**: 362–367.

Nobles, W. W. (1980) *African Psychology* (Oakland, CA: Black Family Institute Publications).

Northcott, M. S. (1992) *The New Age and Pastoral Theology: Towards the Resurgence of the Sacred* (Lightwater, Surrey: Contact Pastoral Trust).

Nouwen, H. (1989) *Seeds of Hope* (London: Darton, Longman and Todd).

Obeyesekere, G. (1984) *Medusa's Hair* (Chicago, IL: University of Chicago Press).

Olds, G. A. (1993) 'The New Age: historic and metaphysical foundations', in D. S. Ferguson (ed.), *New Age Spirituality* (Louisville, Kentucky: Westminster/ John Knox Press).

Oppenheimer, R. (1956) 'Analogy in science', *American Psychologist*, **11**: 127–135.

Pagels, E. (1982) *The Gnostic Gospels* (Harmondsworth: Penguin).

Pahnke, W. N. and Richards, W. A. (1966) 'Implications of LSD and experiential mysticism', *Journal of Religion and Health*, **5**: 176–208.

Palmer, S. and Laungani, P. (eds) (1997) *Counselling in a Multicultural Society* (London: Sage).

Parry, S. J. and Jones, R. G. A. (1996) 'Beyond illusion in the psychotherapeutic enterprise', in G. Claxton (ed.), *Beyond Therapy: The Impact of Eastern Religions on Psychological Theory and Practice* (Dorset: Prism).

Patton, M. Q. (1990) *Qualitative Evaluation and Research Methods* (California: Sage).

Payne, I. R., Bergin, A. E. and Loftus, P. E. (1992) 'A review of attempts to integrate spiritual and standard psychotherapy techniques', *Journal of Psychotherapy Integration*, 2: 171–192.

Peck, M. S. (1990) *The Road Less Travelled, a New Psychology of Love, Traditional Values and Spiritual Growth* (London: Arrow).

Pendzik, S. (1988) 'Drama therapy as a modern form of shamanism', *Journal of Transpersonal Psychology*, 20(1): 81–92.

Peters, L. G. and Price-Williams, D. (1980) 'Towards an experiential analysis of shamanism', *American Ethnologist*, 7: 397–418.

Pietroni, P. (1993) 'The return of the spirit', in A. Beattie, M. Gott, L. Jones. and M. Sidell (eds), *Health and Wellbeing, a Reader* (Milton Keynes: Open University Press).

Polanyi, M. (1962) *Personal Knowledge* (Chicago: University of Chicago Press).

Polkinghorne, D. E. (1992) 'Postmodern epistemology of practice', in S. Kvale (ed.), *Psychology and Postmodernism* (London: Sage).

Pollner, M. (1989) 'Divine relations, social relations, and well-being', *Journal of Health and Social Behavior*, 30: 92–104.

Ponterotto, J. G., Casas, J. M., Suzuki, L. A. and Alexander, C. M. (eds) (1995) *Handbook of Multicultural Counseling* (London: Sage).

Propst, L. R., Ostrom, R., Watkins, P., Dean, T. and Mashburn, D. (1992) 'Comparative efficacy of religious and non-religious cognitive behavioral therapy for the treatment of clinical depression in religious individuals', *Journal of Consulting and Clinical Psychology*, 60: 94–103.

Purcell-Lee, C. and West, W. S. (2000) 'A comparative study into the use of forgiveness in counselling and pastoral care', poster presentation at Society for Psychotherapy research (UK) Annual Conference, Ravenscar, March 2000, 20 January.

Quinn, S. (1987) *A Mind of Her Own: The Life of Karen Horney* (London: Macmillan).

Reason, P. (ed.) (1988) *Human Inquiry in Action* (London: Sage).

Reason, P. (ed.) (1994) *Participation in Human Inquiry* (London: Sage).

Reason, P. and Rowan, J. (eds) (1981) *Human Inquiry, a Sourcebook of New Paradigm Research* (Chichester: John Wiley).

Reich, I. O. (1969) *Wilhelm Reich, a Personal Biography* (New York: St Martin's Press).

Reich, W. (1952) *The Murder of Christ* (New York: Orgone Institute Press).

Rennie, D. L. (1992) 'Qualitative analysis of the client's experience of psychotherapy: the anfolding of reflexivity', in S. G. Joukmanian and D. L. Rennie (eds), *Psychotherapy Process Research: Paradigmatic and Narrative Approaches* (Thousand Oaks, CA: Sage).

Rennie, D. L. (1998) 'Grounded theory methodology: the pressing need for a coherent logic of justification', *Theory and Psychology*, 8(1), 101–119.

Rennie, D. L. (2000) *Anglo-American Qualitative Psychotherapy Research*, 31st Annual Meeting of the Society for Psychotherapy Research (International) Chicago, 22 June.

Rennie, D. L. and Fergus, K. D. (2001) 'It rises from my gut: embodied categorizing in grounded theory analysis', paper to Annual Meeting of the International Society for Theoretical Psychology, Calgary, Alberta, June.

Rennie, D. L., Phillips, J. R. and Quartaro, G. K. (1988) 'Grounded theory: a promising approach to conceptualization in psychology?', *Canadian Psychology*, 29, 139–150.

Richards, D. S. and Bergin, A. E. (eds) (2000) *Handbook of Psychotherapy and Religious Diversity* (Washington, DC: American Psychological Association).

Richards, P. S. and Bergin, A. E. (1997) *A Spiritual Strategy for Counseling and Psychotherapy* (Washington, DC: American Psychological Association).

Richards, W. (1999) 'Rabbits and other outsiders', unpublished paper.

Richards, W. (2002) 'Identity sites: alienation, absence and confusion', paper to the Annual Research Conference of the British Association for Counselling and Psychotherapy, London, May.

Robinson, W. (1997) 'Can we hear one another?', Talk to Quaker Retreat, Savio House, Macclesfield, March.

Rogers, C. R. (1951) *Client-Centred Therapy: Its Current Practice, Implications and Theory* (Boston, MA: Houghton Mifflin).

Rogers, C. R. (1961) *On Becoming a Person* (Boston, MA: Houghton Mifflin).

Rogers, C. R. (1962) 'Some learnings from a study of psychotherapy with schizophrenics', *Pennsylvania Psychiatric Quarterly*, summer issue 3–15.

Rogers, C. R. (1980) *A Way of Being* (Boston, MA: Houghton Mifflin).

Rose, J. (1993) 'The integration of prayer and practice in the counselling relationship', MA thesis, Roehampton Institute of Higher Education.

Rose, J. (1996) *A Needle-Quivering Poise; Between Prayer and Practice in the Counselling Relationship* (Surrey: Contact Pastoral Monograph No. 6).

Rose, J. (2002) *Sharing Spaces? Prayer and the Counselling Relationship* (London: Darton, Longman and Todd).

Rowan, J. (1983) 'The real self and mystical experiences', *Journal of Humanistic Psychology*, 23(2): 9–27.

Rowan, J. (1993) *The Transpersonal, Psychotherapy and Counselling* (London: Routledge).

Rowan, J. (2001) 'Supervision and the psychospiritual levels of development', *Transpersonal Psychology Review*, 5(2): 12–21.

Rye, M. S., Pargament, K. I., Ali, M. A., Beck, G. L., Dorff, E. N., Hallisey, C., Narayanan, V. and Williams, J. G. (2000) 'Religious perspectives on forgiveness', in M. E. McCullough and K. I. Pargament (eds), *Forgiveness: Theory, Research and Practice* (New York: Guildford Press).

Sacks, J. (2002) *The Dignity of Difference* (London: Continuum).

Sands, A. (2000) *Falling for Therapy: Psychotherapy from a Client's Point of View* (London: Macmillan).

Sarbin, T. R. (1986) 'The narrative as a root metaphor for psychology', in T. R. Sarbin (ed.), *Narrative Psychology: The Storied Nature of Human Conduct* (New York: Praeger).

Segal, J. (1992) *Melanie Klein* (London: Sage).

Seymour, E. (1998) 'Towards a pagan/magickal approach to counselling', MSc thesis, University of Bristol.

Shafranske, E. P. (1988) 'The contribution of object relations theory in Christian Counseling', paper presented at the International Convention of Christian Psychology, Atlanta, GA.

Shafranske, E. P. and Malony, H. N. (1985) 'Religion, spirituality, and psychotherapy: a study of Californian psychologists', Paper presented to meeting of the California State Psychological Association, San Francisco, February.

Shafranske, E. P. and Malony, H. N. (1990) 'Clinical psychologists' religious and spiritual orientations and their practice of psychotherapy', *Psychotherapy*, 27(1): 72–78.

Shapiro, D. A., Elliot, R. and Stiles, W. B. (2000) 'Common vs specific factors: a conceptual synthesis', paper to Society for Psychotherapy Research (International) Annual Conference, Chicago, June.

Sharaf, M. (1983) *Fury on Earth, a Biography of Wilhelm Reich* (London: Hutchinson).

Sills, M. (1996) 'Psychotherapy as a spiritual journey', *Self & Society*, 24(4): 7–14.

de Silva, P. (1993) 'Buddhism and Counselling', *British Journal of Guidance and Counselling*, 21(1): 30–34.

de Silva, P. (1996) 'Buddhism and behaviour change: implications for therapy', in G. Claxton (ed.), *Beyond Therapy: The Impact of Eastern Religions on Psychological Theory and Practice* (Dorset: Prism).

Sima, R. G. (2002) 'Possibilities and/or constraints of integrating counselling and traditional healing in Tanzania: the experiences of counsellors and traditional healers', PhD thesis, University of Manchester.

Skovholt, T. M. and Ronnestad, M. H. (1992) *The Evolving Professional Self, Stages and Themes in Therapist and Counselor Development* (Chichester: John Wiley & Sons).

Sollod, R. N. (1978) 'Carl Rogers and the origins of client-centred therapy', *Professional Psychology*, 9: 93–104.

Spangler, D. (1993) 'The New Age: movement towards the divine', in D. S. Ferguson (ed.), *New Age Spirituality* (Louisville, Kentucky: Westminster/John Knox Press).

Spanos, I. (1978) 'Witchcraft in histories of psychiatry: a critical analysis and alternative conceptualisation', *Psychological Bulletin*, 85: 417–439.

Stoltenberg, C. D. and Delworth, U. (1988) *Supervising Counselors and Therapists* (London: Jossey-Bass).

Strauss, A. and Corbin J. (1990) *Basics of Qualitative Research: Grounded Theory Procedures and Techniques* (London: Sage).

Strupp, H. H. (1972) 'On the technology of psychotherapy', *Archives of General Psychiatry*, **26**: 270–278.

Sue, D. W. and Sue, D. (1990) *Counselling the Culturally Different*, 2nd edition (New York: John Wiley & Sons).

Summers, R. (1997) 'Glimpsing something of the spirit', *Friends Quarterly*, **30**(7): 328–332.

Swinton, J. (2001) *Spirituality and Mental Health Care, Rediscovering a 'Forgotten' Dimension* (London: Jessica Kingsley).

Swinton, V. (1996) 'A study of the attitudes to the exploration of spiritual awareness in counselling training', MA thesis, Department of Applied Social Studies, Keele University.

Symington, N. (1994) *Emotion and Spirit; Questioning the Claims of Psychoanalysis and Religion* (London: Cassell).

Szasz, T. (1988) *The Myth of Psychotherapy* (New York: Syracuse University Press).

Tart, C. T. and Deikman, A. J. (1991) 'Mindfulness, spiritual seeking and psychotherapy', *Journal of Transpersonal Psychology*, **23**(1): 29–52.

Thomas, L. E. and Cooper, P. E. (1980) 'Incidence and psychological correlates of intense spiritual experiences', *Journal of Transpersonal Psychology*, **12**(1): 75–85.

Thoresen, C. E., Luskin, F. and Harris, A. H. S. (1998) 'Science and forgiveness interventions: reflections and recommendations', in E. L. Worthington, Jr (ed.), *Dimensions of Forgiveness, Psychological Research and Theological Perspectives* (London: Templeton Foundation).

Thorne, B. (1988) 'Psychotherapy and original sin', *Self and Society*, **16**(5): 207–214.

Thorne, B. (1991) *Person-Centred Counselling: Therapeutic and Spiritual Dimensions* (London: Whurr).

Thorne, B. (1992) *Carl Rogers* (London: Sage).

Thorne, B. (1994) 'Developing a spiritual discipline', in D. Mearns (ed.), *Developing Person-Centred Counselling*, pp. 44–47 (London: Sage).

Thorne, B. (1998) *Person-Centred Counselling and Christian Spirituality: The Secular and the Holy* (London: Whurr).

Thorne, B. (2002) *The Mystical Power of Person-Centred Therapy* (London: Whurr).

Tick, E. (1992) 'Attending the soul', *Voices*, **28**(2): 7–8.

Toulmin, S. (1990) *Cosmopolis: The Hidden Agenda of Modernity* (Chicago: University of Chicago Press).

Towler, R. (1974) *Homo Religious* (London: Constable).

Tseng, W. and Hsu, J. (1979) 'Culture and psychotherapy', in A. J. Marsella, R. Thorp and T. Ciborowski (eds), *Perspectives on Cross-Cultural Psychology* (New York: Academic Press).

Tsu, Lao (1963) *Tao Te Ching*, translated by D. C. Lau (Penguin: Harmondsworth).

Tune, D. (2001) 'Is touch a valid therapeutic intervention? Early returns from a qualitative study of therapists' views', *Counselling and Psychotherapy Research*, **1(1)**: 167–171.

Valla, J.-P. and Prince, R. H. (1990) 'Religious experiences as self-healing mechanisms', in C. A. Ward (ed.), *Altered States of Consciousness and Mental Health, a Cross-Cultural Perspective* (California: Sage).

Van Belle, H. A. (1990) 'Rogers' later move towards mysticism, implications for client-centred therapy', in G. Lietaer and R. Van Balen (eds), *Client-Centred and Experiential Psychotherapy in the Nineties* (The Netherlands: University of Leuven).

Vaughan, F. (1986) *The Inward Arc, Healing and Wholeness in Psychotherapy and Spirituality* (California: Shambhala).

Vaughan, F. (1989) 'True and false mystical experiences', *Revision*, **12**: 4–10.

Vaughan, F. (1991) 'Spiritual issues in psychotherapy', *Journal of Transpersonal Psychology*, **23(2)**: 105–119.

Veness, D. (1990) 'Spirituality in counselling: a view from the other side', *British Journal of Guidance & Counselling*, **18(3)**: 250–260.

Vigne, J. (1991) 'Guru and psychotherapist: comparisons from the Hindu tradition', *Journal of Transpersonal Psychology*, **23(2)**: 121–137.

Vitz, P. (1993) *Sigmund Freud's Christian Unconscious* (Grand Rapids, Mich.: Eerdmans).

Walker, A. (1998) *Restoring the Kingdom, the Radical Christianity of the House Church Movement* (Guildford: Eagle).

Wallis, J. H. (1993) *Findings; An Inquiry into Quaker Religious Experience* (London: Quaker Home Service).

Walsh, R. (1989) 'What is a shamen?', *Journal of Transpersonal Psychology*, **21(1)**: 1–11.

Walsh, R. (1994) 'The making of a shaman: calling, training and culmination', *Journal of Humanistic Psychology*, **34(3)**: 7–30.

Walsh, R. and Vaughan, F. (1994) 'The worldview of Ken Wilber', *Journal of Humanistic Psychology*, **34(2)**: 6–21.

Ward, E., King, M., Lloyd, M., Bower, P., Sibbald, B., Farelly, S., Gabbay, M., Tarrier, N. and Addington-Hall, J. (2000) 'Randomised controlled trial of non-directive counselling, cognitive-behaviour therapy, and usual general practitioner care for patients with depression. I: Clinical effectiveness', *British Medical Journal*, **321(7273)**: 1383–1388.

Washburn, M. (1990) 'Two patterns of transcendence', *Journal of Humanistic Psychology*, **30(3)**: 84–112.

Watson, K. W. (1994) 'Spiritual emergency: concepts and implications for psychotherapy', *Journal of Humanistic Psychology*, **34(2)**: 22–45.

Watts, A. (1961) *Psychotherapy East and West* (New York: Pantheon Books).

West, W. S. (1985) *Loving Contact* (Leeds: Energy Stream Publications).

West, W. S. (1988) *Melting Armour* (Leeds: Energy Stream publications).

West, W. S. (1994a) 'Clients experience of bodywork psychotherapy', *Counselling Psychology Quarterly*, **7**(3): 287–303.

West, W. S. (1994b) 'Post Reichian Therapy', in D. Jones (ed.), *Innovative Therapy: A Handbook* (Buckingham: Open University Press).

West, W. S. (1995a) 'Integrating Psychotherapy and Healing: an Inquiry into the Experiences of Counsellors and Psychotherapists Whose Work Includes Healing' PhD thesis, University of Keele.

West, W. S. (1995b) 'The relevance of Quakerism for counsellors', *The Friends Quarterly*, **28**(5): 22–226.

West, W. S. (1996) 'Using human inquiry groups in counselling research', *British Journal of Guidance and Counselling*, **24**(3): 347–355.

West, W. S. (1997) 'Integrating Psychotherapy and healing', *British Journal of Guidance and Counselling*, **25**(3): 291–312.

West, W. S. (1998a) 'Developing practice in a context of religious faith: a study of psychotherapists who are Quakers', *British Journal of Guidance & Counselling*, **26**(3): 365–375.

West, W. S. (1998b) 'Therapy as a spiritual process', in C. Feltham (ed.), *Witness and Vision of Therapists*, pp. 158–179 (London: Sage).

West, W. S. (1998c) 'Critical subjectivity: use of self in counselling research', *Counselling*, **9**(3): 228–230.

West, W. S. (1998d) 'Spirituality and work', *Friends Quarterly*, **31**(3): 138–142.

West, W. S. (1998e) 'Passionate research, heuristics and the use of self in counselling research', *Changes*, **16**(1): 60–66.

West, W. S. (1999) 'Counselling as a spiritual space', *Counselling and Creation*, proceedings of the 6th Annual International Counselling Conference, Durham: School of Education, Durham University.

West, W. S. (2000a) *Psychotherapy and Spirituality: Crossing the Line between Therapy and Religion* (London: Sage).

West, W. S. (2000b) 'Supervision difficulties and dilemmas for counsellors and psychotherapists around healing and spirituality', in B. Lawton and C. Feltham (eds), *Taking Supervision Forward: Dilemmas, Insights and Trends* (London: Sage).

West, W. S. (2000c) 'Eclecticism and integration in humanistic therapy', in S. Palmer and R. Woolfe (eds), *Eclectic and Integrative Counselling and Psychotherapy* (London: Sage).

West, W. S. (2000d) 'Issues relating to the use of forgiveness in psychotherapy', paper presented to the Society for Psychotherapy Research (International) Annual Conference, Chicago, 23 June.

West, W. S. (2000e) 'Some of my spiritual experiences', *The Friends Quarterly*, **32**(1): 16–19.

West, W. S. (2001a) 'Issues relating to the use of forgiveness in counseling and psychotherapy', *British Journal of Guidance and Counselling*, **29**(4): 415–423.

West, W. S. (2001b) 'Retreats', *Newsletter of the Association for Pastoral and Spiritual Care and Counselling*, August, pp. 6–7.

West, W. S. (2001c) 'Counselling, psychotherapy and religion', in S. Spooner-King and C. Newnes (eds), *Spirituality and Psychotherapy*, pp. 5–10 (Ross-on-Wye: PCCS Books).

West, W. S. (2001d) 'Beyond grounded theory: the use of a heuristic approach to qualitative research', *Counselling Psychotherapy Research*, 1(2): 126–131.

West, W. S. (2002a) 'Some ethical dilemmas in counselling and counselling research', *British Journal of Guidance and Counselling*, 30(3): 261–268.

West, W. S. (2002b) 'Being present to our clients' spirituality', *Journal of Critical Psychology, Counselling and Psychotherapy*, 2(2): 86–93.

West, W. S. (2003a) 'The culture of psychotherapy supervision', *Counselling Psychotherapy Research*, 3(2): 123–128.

West, W. S. (2003b) 'Humanistic integrative spiritual therapy with a Sufi convert', in D. S. Richards and A. E. Bergin (eds), *A Casebook for a Spiritual Strategy in Counseling and Psychotherapy* (Washington, DC: American Psychological Association).

West, W. S. and Mansor, A. T. (2002) 'Hearing what research participants are really saying: the influence of research cultural identity', *Counselling and Psychotherapy Research*, 2(4): 253–258.

West, W. S. and McLeod, J. (2003) 'Cultural landscapes in counselling and psychotherapy: introduction to the Theme Section', *Counselling and Psychotherapy Research*, 3(2): 83–86.

Whitmore, D. (1996) 'The psychospiritual and the transpersonal', *Self & Society*, 24(4): 26–29.

Wilber, K. (1975) 'Psychologia Perennis: the spectrum of consciousness', *Journal of Transpersonal Psychology*, 7(2): 105–132.

Wilber, K. (1979a) 'Eye to eye, the relationship between science, reason and religion and its affect on transpersonal psychology', *Revision*, winter/spring, pp. 3–26.

Wilber, K. (1979b) 'A developmental view of consciousness', *Journal of Transpersonal Psychology*, 11(1): 1–21.

Wilber, K. (1980) *The Atman Project* (Illinois: Quest).

Wilber, K. (1983) *A Sociable God, Towards a New Understanding of Religion* (Boulder, Colorado: Shambhala).

Wilber, K. (1990) 'Two patterns of transcendence, a reply to Washburn', *Journal of Humanistic Psychology*, 30(3): 113–136.

Wilber, K. (2001a) *Grace and Grit: Spirituality and Healing in the Life and Death of Treya Killam Wilber* (Dublin: Gateway).

Wilber, K. (2001b) *A Theory of Everything: An Integral Vision for Business, Politics, Science and Spirituality* (Dublin: Gateway).

Willis, R. (1992a) 'Initiation into healing', *Doctor-Healer Network Newsletter*, 3: 9–11.

Willis, R. (1992b) 'What makes a healer?', *International Journal of Alternative and Complementary Medicine*, November, p. 11.

Wilson, A. (1993) *The Falsification of Afrikan Consciousness* (New York: African World Info Systems).

Wilson, B. R. (ed.) (1981) *The Social Impact of New Religious Movements* (New York: Rose of Sharon Press).

Winkelman, M. (1989) 'A cross-cultural study of shamanic healers', *Journal of Psychoactive Drugs*, 21: 17–24.

Worthington, E. L. (ed.) (1998) *Dimensions of Forgiveness: Psychological Research and Theological Perspectives* (London: Templeton).

Wosket, V. (1999) *The Therapeutic Use of Self: Counselling Practice, Research and Supervision* (London: Routledge).

Yalom, I. D. (1980) *Existential Psychotherapy* (New York: Basic Books).

Young, C. (1988) 'New Age Spirituality', *Self & Society*, 16(5): 195–201.

Index